The Crossword Solver's Guide

May Abbott

A DAILY TELEGRAPH BOOK

Collins London and Glasgow

First published 1975

© May Abbott and the *Daily Telegraph* 1975

ISBN 0 00 412044 2

Printed in Great Britain by
Wm Collins Sons & Co Ltd, London & Glasgow

Contents

I

The Invisible Opponent

'I enjoy doing the Quick Crossword every day – but I do wish I could do the big one. The trouble is I simply can't make head or tail of any of the clues!'

This tale of woe is not at all unusual, yet anybody who can solve straightforward crossword puzzles should be able to tackle, and enjoy, the cryptic ones. It is simply a question of getting the knack of unravelling the clues.

For instance, if any complete novice were to turn now to page 12 and study the first Test Word's clues his or her first reaction would probably be: 'Oh, I'm not clever enough to do *that*!' Yet I can guarantee that any beginner, after reading chapter 2, will be able to solve that Test Word in a few minutes.

The style, standard and degree of difficulty of puzzles will be seen to vary greatly in different publications, and the latter may lay down their own 'rules'. But the only 'rule' which normally applies to all is that the compiler must provide a set of fair clues which must be capable of being worked out accurately. The clues must never be based on errors of fact, nor must the compiler 'cheat' by relying on facts which it would be impossible for his solvers to know.

Within the general framework of crossword puzzles we may expect to see any words found in a standard dictionary, idioms and figures of speech, acceptable colloquial words, slang, or modern words in general use, and proper nouns, whether the names of people, places or things. Compilers are apt to seize on the most unusual meanings of everyday words, so we should check our dictionaries very carefully before writing off to the Editor to point out the mistake in his crossword! Puzzles often contain references to topical events or to people in the news, from politics to sport, all of which helps to keep the puzzles lively and interesting.

Some cryptic crosswords are so intricate and erudite that many solvers have to keep returning to them over several days before completing them. They are for the advanced puzzlers, and are beyond the scope of this book. Here we shall concentrate on the type of puzzles which appear in daily and Sunday newspapers and informed periodicals and which the average commuter should be able to finish during train journeys or lunch breaks.

We should look on our crossword not so much as a 'puzzle for one' as a 'game for two'.

The compiler is our opponent, invisible, but very real. He is the friendliest challenger we shall ever meet, for *he wants us to win* . . . in the end. However cunningly he may fox us with his word-play, he knows that if he should prove to be too clever for the majority of his contestants then he, paradoxically, is the loser.

For the average cryptic puzzle each clue the compiler writes usually does two things:

(a) it contains a definition or description (either written or implied) telling us what the answer *is*;

(b) it provides us with a secondary clue (or clue within a clue) telling us something *about* the answer.

The *definition* might comprise just one word or phrase somewhere within the clue, or it might be one of two or more possible meanings of the entire clue.

The *secondary clue*, the 'embroidery', is the part which gives the compiler the most fun and which challenges his, and our, ingenuity. Again, it may be a word or phrase within the clue, or another meaning of the entire clue.

We, as solvers, must learn to recognize which part of the clue is which. We must also be ever ready to take everything the compiler says quite literally. Once we have trained ourselves to do that we will clear the biggest single hurdle that defeats beginners. Just how to take him literally we will see in later chapters.

By the end of chapter 15 we should be able to tackle the average cryptic crossword puzzle with reasonable confidence and enjoyment. Complete success every time may follow.

As we work our way through the chapters it will become clear that there are many accepted crossword 'conventions'. Regular solvers, over the years, amass a considerable store of crossword know-how and acquire a fair idea of how the compiler's brain ticks; the compiler, in turn, is always seeking fresh ways and new turns of phrase to outwit them.

The old hands, who can polish off a puzzle in less than half an hour, know by heart the innumerable abbreviations which so often recur, the short syllables, the gymnastics of letters, the subtle meanings of apparently simple words.

The glossary at the end of this book, which lists many of these 'conventions', is designed to help to put the beginner on a level with the old hands. It is *not* intended as a 'crib' to provide instant solutions to difficult clues!

2

Hidden Words

We are tackling our first cryptic crossword puzzle. We have read through all the clues, and every one has left us stumped.

Let us go through them again. The compiler may have slipped in one or two easy clues to give us a start while at the same time disguising them to make them *look* difficult. The answers might be staring us in the face, literally printed in black and white on the page: they are 'hidden words'.

A hidden solution may comprise one or more words, and is spelt out in the clue in correct consecutive order. Identifying it is made easier if we remember that in a cryptic puzzle every clue ends with a figure in brackets telling us how many letters there are in the answer. If the latter is made up of two or more words the number of letters in *each* word will be shown like this: (5,3,8).

Here is an elementary example of a 'hidden word':

Item of furniture in Constable's house (5)
answer: table

How and why have we come to such an answer? Remembering that the clue should give us a definition of the complete solution we will begin by assuming that here it is 'item of furniture'. If so, the secondary clue is confined to the three words 'in Constable's house'.

What is the compiler trying to tell us in his piece of 'embroidery'? When he refers to 'Constable' does he mean a policeman? Or the British landscape painter? And what item of furniture might we find in a policeman's or artist's home that we would not expect to find in a lawyer's or a greengrocer's, for instance?

These are indeed the questions an alert solver should ask himself . . . but already the compiler is leading us up the garden. For the answer lies in none of these things, but in our readiness to read the clue *literally*. If we take the preposition 'in' literally we find that item of furniture printed in the phrase 'Cons*table*'s house'.

Very few clues are as obvious as this. However, if we analyse the method in detail we will learn how to unearth more subtly buried 'hidden words' later on. Following this principle of hiding the answer in the clue the compiler could have written

> *Item of furniture in stable yard* (5)

but he would be very unlikely to do so. Why? Because although structurally accurate (the letters t–a–b–l–e being *in* the clue) the total meaning of the clue and answer would be sloppy, a non-sequitur of the type a compiler will avoid if he possibly can.

Just to get the 'feel' of such simple hidden word clues, here are a few more examples:

> *Card game in abridged form* (5)
> answer: bridge
> *Listeners within earshot* (4)
> answer: ears
> *Shape inside information* (4)
> answer: form

Note how the words 'in', 'within' and 'inside' have tipped us off to look for the solution hidden in the clues. Such easy clues would soon become boring, however, so the compiler may make them less obvious by using synonyms.

Reverting to the first example, the 'item of furniture', the puzzle setter might choose a different definition for 'table', using it in the sense of an arrangement of facts and figures to make a timetable, a rota of duties, a synopsis of scientific facts, or a multiplication table. It might properly be defined as a 'tabulation', a 'list', an 'index', 'syllabus' or 'schedule'. Even the item of furniture could be defined as a 'board'. Again, a table might be an 'inscribed tablet'.

If the compiler decided to substitute 'index' (a table of reference) for 'item of furniture' the clue would become

Index found in Constable's house (5)

which would be another unsatisfactory non-sequitur, the sense of the first clue having been lost. Substitute

Index in constable's rule-book (5)

and again the whole makes sense; it has a definition of the answer, while 'in' leads us to the hidden word.

In time we will look for more subtle secondary clues. Instead of being told that the answer is *in* the clue we may be given the mere hint that it is 'displayed', 'shown' or 'caught' in it. Our last example might now become

Whitstable displays index (5)

Now that last example, where the 'embroidery' comes first and the definition last, has moved a long way from the item of furniture in Constable's house. Here are a few words and phrases *of the kind* that might indicate a 'hidden word' clue:

discloses	includes	a feature of
swallows	harbours	buried in
contained	enmeshes	veiled by
takes in	lurks in	part of
helps to make	seen in	constituent of

Again, we must remember to read the clues literally, so that one set of letters, or word, is in, or forms part of, a phrase. Here are some more illustrations of 'hidden word' clues: identify the definition in each, and spot where the solution is printed:

Cat buried in *tomb* (3)
answer: *Tom*
A carrier trapped in *betrayal* (4)
answer: *tray*

Fashion hidden in *modesty* (4)
answer: mode
Pamphlet obscured by *distractions* (5)
answer: tract

May be seen puffing inside when it rains

In all the examples so far, the 'hidden word' has been held within one word of the clue. But the compiler might camouflage his solution to make it form part of a phrase – always providing, of course, that the letters follow in correct, unbroken sequence. Thus:

Laying up stores in Bostock in groups (8)
answer: stocking

At first glance this looks a really tough clue. But that little 'in', plus the somewhat contrived phraseology, should make us *look* for a 'hidden word'. (This is not to say that 'in' *always* implies a hidden solution – far from it!) In this case, there it is, in '. . . Bo*stock in* groups'. So 'laying up stores' defines the answer, 'stocking', which is hidden in the secondary clue. Again:

Up and away, catching an animal (5)
answer: panda

There is a difference of construction here. We have the secondary clue first, 'U*p and a*way' catching, or trapping, the word 'panda'. Its definition, an animal, comes at the end of the clue. There is no rule to say that a definition must come first and its 'embroidery' must follow. We must learn to look anywhere for the solution's definition.

> *Sailor's ketch upended; some sauce!* (7)
> *answer: ketchup*

Here we have another clue with the definition at the end, i.e. 'sauce'. The hint of a 'hidden word' here is 'some'. We are being told that *some* of the clue means 'sauce', and it does not take long to find it in 'sailor's *ketch up*ended'.

Sometimes punctuation marks are used to mask a 'hidden word' more effectively. They improve the way the whole clue reads, but it is often helpful to ignore them when looking for the hidden answer. Like this:

> *Pop, ill, soon swallows tablets* (5)
> *answer: pills*

Again the definition, 'tablets', is at the end of the clue. The first part of the clue 'swallows' the answer – and it is easier to find it if we ignore the commas – hidden in 'Po*p, ill, s*oon'.

> *Makes haste although showing furtiveness* (7)
> *answer: stealth*

Note how the words 'makes ha*ste alth*ough' are literally *showing* 'stealth', or furtiveness.

> *Pitt read millionaire a tract exposing slave drudgery* (9)
> *answer: treadmill*

The solution is exposed in 'Pit*t read mill*ionaire . . .' In a nutshell, a 'hidden answer' is easily found in any clue, once you know it's there. The real art is in identifying the clues in which such solutions are hidden.

Few cryptic puzzles would be likely to contain more than one or two such clues. However, we have looked at them at length because they make a good initiation into the cryptic 'mysteries' which turn out to be not so mysterious!

Our first Test Word is made up entirely of 'hidden word' clues, so it should be possible to solve it fairly quickly. In doing so the really important thing is to make sure that

(a) we have understood how the definition and the secondary clue relate to the 'hidden word', and

(b) if we saw each clue in a real crossword puzzle we would recognize it as one probably 'hiding' the answer.

Test Word 1

(Solution on page 98)

Across

1 The best ringers hold the cord (6)
4 Cot displayed amid exotic ribbons (4)
7 Redcar petshop has warm floor covering (6)
8 Kind of dwelling in S E Mitcham? (4)
10 What pal thought exposed, notwithstanding (8)
13 Massacre's set scene includes torches (8)
16 Piranha's country? (4)
17 Noah's posh ark shelters vicious fish (6)
18 A nasty cut in the strong ash tree (4)
19 Contents of big rate demand jarred (6)

Down

1 Crooks acknowledged hiding the bag (4)
2 Red and rather raw in the Tundra region (4)
3 Wasters need lesson showing what's unnecessary (8)
5 Sorry part of true fulfilment (6)
6 Bob, right ahead, shining in there! (6)
9 Seen in his best hat, Cherwell's rural craftsman (8)
11 Stage performance in tact in Garden Theatre (6)
12 Limpet also swallows parts of blossoms (6)
14 Jog along in Trotsky style (4)
15 Second-hand refuse Don buries (4)

3

Multiple Definitions

Another type of fairly simple clue is the double definition. The clue is basically similar to many of the clues used regularly in 'quick' or primitive puzzles. The latter, we remember, usually consist of one or two straightforward synonyms or descriptions of the solutions. For example, in a 'quick' puzzle we might find this:

Clue		Solution
1	*coarse*	*gross*
2	*copper*	*constable*
3	*bestow*	*grant*
4	*captain*	*skipper*
5	*product*	*yield*

The only real problem that this kind of clue presents is that it is *too* simple. Many words in the English language have so many different meanings that there could be more than one correct answer to fit the space allowed. The main problem becomes one of choosing a word which will interlock with the others. For the same set of sample solutions above, we might see these clues:

Clue		Solution
1	*twelve dozen*	*gross*
2	*an artist*	*Constable*
3	*allowance*	*grant*
4	*hopper*	*skipper*
5	*surrender*	*yield*

The cryptic puzzle takes these clues a stage further. It uses two together. So when the pairs are 'married' they turn out like this:

Clue	Solution
1 *coarse twelve dozen*	*gross*
2 *copper artist*	*Constable*
3 *bestow allowance*	*grant*
4 *Captain Hopper*	*skipper*
5 *surrender product*	*yield*

We see at once that the sense of each clue is changed. A 'copper artist' might suggest the name of some great etcher; 'Captain Hopper' might be a famous personality from fact or fiction like 'Captain Cook' or 'Captain Bligh', so we search our memory for his Christian name, and so on.

The simplest words may not only have several meanings, some as nouns, others as verbs; they may also have unusual meanings, and we must always look for these as well.

'Butter', at first glance, means a dairy product. But it is also used as 'flattery', or, as a verb, to 'butter somebody up'. And it can mean 'an animal that butts' – e.g., a goat. Compilers are fond of picking on the *least expected* meanings for their words; a 'four-legged butter' is a good example.

Thus, our first reaction to 'a bloomer' would be to think of a howler, a mistake, dropping a brick. A compiler might prefer to use it in the sense of 'something that blooms' e.g., a rose bush or a daisy plant.

Similarly, 'a flower' to the compiler may mean 'something that flows' – i.e., a river. Who can argue that the Thames and the Severn are not 'flowers'? 'Summer', in addition to being a season, may be 'one who sums up' or an 'adder'. Conversely, an 'adder' may be a 'summer' as well as being a snake!

Couldn't a 'revolver' be a turnstile, a record player, the world? A 'howler' could be a bloomer or schoolboy mistake, but it might also be a dog, a jackal, or a discontented baby. A 'number' could be something that numbs: an injection? Double definitions for these words might make clues something like this:

Clue	Solution
1 *fat goat*	*butter*
2 *summer snake*	*adder*
3 *Amazon blossom*	*flower*

Again, these clues might momentarily have put us off the scent. We might have searched our brains for some fat old Aries, or for a serpent that turns up in the summer but not in the spring or autumn, or for some exotic bloom from South America.

Discipline retinue

Before we move on to a more elaborate form of double definition let us take one more look at our eight simple examples. Suppose the compiler had separated his definitions with commas (as he would have done for a 'quick' puzzle). We would see this:

	Clue	Solution
1	*coarse, twelve dozen*	*gross*
2	*copper, artist*	*constable*
3	*bestow, allowance*	*grant*
4	*captain, hopper*	*skipper*
5	*surrender, product*	*yield*
6	*fat, goat*	*butter*
7	*summer, snake*	*adder*
8	*Amazon, blossom*	*flower*

Immediately we are back to the simple definitions. The linked meanings have gone. There is an obvious lesson to be learned from this:

Insert imaginary commas into short clues to see if they turn into 'double definitions'.

We have discussed 'double definitions', but in fact if he can manage it our compiler may well give us a treble definition as his clue. When the words are drawn from verbs, nouns and adjectives the result can put us off the scent completely. 'Concern' may mean to involve; it may refer to a business establishment; or it may, among other things, mean worry or anxiety. Strung together in a row:

Involve business anxiety

the effect can be somewhat formidable! But punctuate it, in the mind's eye, with commas, to read:

Involve, business, anxiety

and the clue becomes quite manageable.

So far we have looked at double and treble definitions where each word consists of *one* word only. But the compiler may extend this type of clue by using phrases, probably of two or three words each, instead of single words. The result is that we have a clue which reads more smoothly, says something more interesting, and is altogether more mystifying. For example:

The elderly are making progress going aboard (7,2)

Too many words here to divide with imaginary commas; we substitute imaginary bars. A few experiments could produce:

The elderly are/making progress/going aboard

Now we have found three definitions for 'getting on' which is the correct answer. (The fact that we knew that its second word had only two letters should have helped.) Again:

Little bit of waste scrimmage (5)

By putting in imaginary divisions we pretend we see

Little bit of/waste/scrimmage

and we soon decide that 'scrap' fits all three. Look at

Tar to establish a musical key (5)

and convert this to—

Tar/to establish/a musical key
answer: pitch
Boot Napoleon's adversary in Shropshire (9)
answer: Wellington

(i.e., Wellington boot/ the Duke of Wellington/ the Shropshire town of Wellington).

It would be readily agreed that many of the above examples read in a clumsy way. Sometimes compilers tackle this problem of 'jerkiness' in the clue by linking two definitions together with a preposition such as 'and', 'with' etc.

To revert to one of the earlier examples – 'Captain Hopper'. The compiler could with fairness alter it (though he would be unlikely to) so as to read,

> *Captain and hopper* (7)
> *answer: skipper*

because a 'skipper' can mean a captain *and* it can mean a hopper. Indeed, it would be fair to go further, like this:

> *Captain Hopper, one who passes over* (7)

Here the clue has acquired a third definition, namely a person who may 'skip' something, such as reading a page, or a duty, or a visit to be paid.

When it comes to pairing longer definitions the linking preposition makes a much improved clue. Examples:

> *A bore for soldiers' exercise* (5)
> *answer: drill*
> *A sharp tug for the American* (4)
> *answer: Yank*
> *Allowed to go and not made to pay* (3,3)
> *answer: let off*

The most interesting multiple definition clues are often those where one meaning is literal and another is metaphorical – a figure of speech or a colloquialism. A simple illustration: 'In the soup'. Literally, lentils, or noodles, or croutons may be in the soup; figuratively so can somebody who is in a spot of bother. 'Up to a point' may mean 'so far, in an argument'. But it can also have a physical interpretation; a fir tree may be said to grow 'up to a point'. These may be more difficult to solve for the beginner, and we will be returning to this type later in this book, but here are a few examples of clues which fall into this category:

> *Transported to work and called to account* (5,2,4)
> *answer: taken to task*
> *Forget old quarrels and put on a new face* (4,2)
> *answer: make up*
> *A jolly fine person, one who stops up bottlenecks?* (1,6)
> *answer: a corker*
> *A betrayal for a packed house* (4–3)
> *answer: sell-out*

Test Word 2

(Solution on page 99)

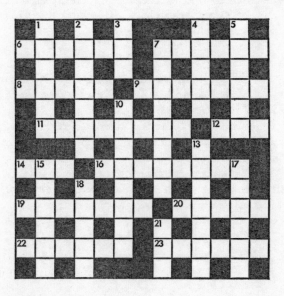

Across

6 Written message permitter (6)
7 Twine the stable's racehorses (6)
8 Coarse Yankee woman loved by Norfolk boatmen (5)
9 More candid marker (7)
11 Unusually big beating (8)
12 Pig pen eye sore (3)
14 Urge an Easter gift (3)
16 Disposed to be slanted (8)
19 Drank to warmly browned (7)
20 Clumsily move river freight boat (5)
22 Furtively passes tale tellers (6)
23 Policeman stripper (6)

Down

1 Search out a polecat (6)
2 Social grade layer (7)
3 Sizzle the poet Christopher (3)
4 Faddist engine turner (5)
5 Lay out money to besiege (6)

7   Powerfully with concentration (8)
10 Wipers-up parasites (8)
13 Affianced busily occupied (7)
15 Solid land crushed to powder (6)
17 New Zealand miner excavator (6)
18 Attempt a written composition (5)
21 Spot agent (3)

4

Anagrams

An anagram is a word or phrase made up of *all* the letters of another word or phrase. 'Pin' is an anagram of 'nip', 'creator' of 'reactor', 'sprite's tea' of 'strip tease', and so on.

Some people love solving anagrams; others loathe them. There are solvers who have only to look at an anagram for its component letters to sort themselves out, apparently by themselves, into the required new order; there are others who need to make lengthy scribblings in the margins of their newspapers, scribbling the letters in various orders, before they find the right solution.

(A tip for beginners: a set of letters taken from a Lexicon pack or a Scrabble game can be useful for trying out re-arrangements of an anagram.)

Like 'hidden words' and double definitions, anagrams can be very useful for giving us a start on a puzzle. We can do worse than comb through the clues looking for the obvious ones. They fall into two categories: stated anagrams, and disguised anagrams.

1. Stated anagrams
Most of us are familiar with this straightforward type of clue:

Bustle (anag.) (6)

It doesn't take much juggling around with the letters to come up with the word 'subtle'. Or again:

Fringe (anag.) (6)

We soon turn that into 'finger'. On rare occasions the compiler might invite us to make a word from a meaningless row of letters, like this,

cchipsu (anag.) (7)

and we might need quite a few tries before coming up with 'hiccups'. An anagram could be made up into two or more words, thus:

Miser sped (anag.) (9)
answer: impressed
Pelt ash (anag.) (4,3)
answer: the Alps
Apt peeler (anag.) (5,4)
answer: apple tree

Such bald statements, however, are not very interesting. Indeed, when the anagram becomes overlong – say, one of 10 letters or more – it can become difficult or boring to solve without a secondary clue. And this is what the compiler of a cryptic puzzle invariably gives us. To take the last two examples again, this is how he might deal with them:

Pelt ash (anag.) (Though they're not volcanic!) (3,4)

Now this extra comment suggests that we might expect the answer to be something volcanic since 'they' throw ash about the place. Some sort of mountain, perhaps? A much more interesting way to arrive at 'the Alps'!

Apt peeler (anag.) (Where there are windfalls?) (5,4)

The aside, in brackets, immediately suggests a link between 'peeling' and 'fruit', helping us more speedily to find the solution, 'apple tree'.

So in cryptic puzzles there are usually two factors to help us solve anagrams – the compiler's comment about it, and the number of letters in each word.

The small words can be a big help. 'And', 'the', 'in', 'on' and suchlike are easily detected as a rule. But even with a two-letter word in the phrase, this anagram might take some time to solve—

Brusque to idol (6,2,5)

– because there's nothing to give us a lead. But when the compiler has added his aside, like this—

> *Brusque to idol (anag.) (Last gamble involved?)* (6,2,5)

– he suggests that the answer has something to do with taking a chance, with laying a bet, and – by the word 'last' – that it's something to do with a sequence of chances. Hence, 'double or quits'.

> *Ho! Given land! (anag.) (Oho! close co-operation!)* (4,2,5)

The echoing exclamation, Oho! suggests there might be something fishy here, a little bit of scheming together, perhaps? The words that follow clinch the answer: 'Hand in glove'.

In order to get into the compiler's mind let us swop places with him for a moment. We have a solution, 'One for the pot', and we want to make a clue based on its anagram. What choice do we have from the constituent letters? Possibly

> *On top, thereof*
> *Free hot pot? No!*
> *Ten of the poor*
> *Top of the Nore*
> *Note the proof*

Which of these might make the most *apt* association with 'One for the pot'? We are dealing with an age-old, traditional formula for making the standard British 'cuppa', a stimulating non-alcoholic drink. We would probably select the last anagram, because that too has an association with liquid refreshment (though alcoholic) and the phrase *runs freely* with the solution. Our clue might read:

> *Note the proof (anag.) (It makes a stronger drink!)* (3,3,3,3)

Here we have made a clue which, with its solution, tells a story: 'The proof of the measure of putting an extra spoonful in the pot is that you get a stronger cup of tea.' (At the same time, were we in the compiler's shoes, we would enjoy leading our solver up the garden a little here, because the first reaction to the association of 'proof' with 'strong drink' is that it must relate to alcohol.)

To repeat the exercise, suppose we want to make an

anagram clue for 'mountain-sides'. These letters lend themselves to many promising combinations, but for a start we might make:

> *So I'm in sad tune*
> *Dim aunt's noise*
> *O.S. maid tunes in*
> *Sonia's dim tune*
> *S.O.S. I am tuned in*

Remembering that we want to have some plausible connection with the mountains the first and last anagrams seem to be the most promising. 'So I'm in sad tune' might be made to link up with yodellers, perhaps, or somebody playing an alpenhorn? But for a more subtle development we might select

> *S.O.S. I am tuned in* (anag.) (*High hopes dashed on them?*) (8-5)

The appeal for help in the anagram suggests somebody in distress, tuned in to their radio awaiting rescue. The secondary clue suggests, both literally and figuratively, an effort to fly or climb 'high'. While ordinary hopes might be dashed by rocks, reefs, stumbling-blocks, high ones will come to grief on . . . mountain-sides.

Looking back over the examples in this chapter so far, we will find one thing in common to all the clues: they all *stated* the answer was an anagram. We knew exactly what we were looking for. Now we turn to less obvious examples.

2. Disguised anagrams

Instead of baldly *stating* that the answer is an anagram of a word or words, in the clue the compiler tells us in a roundabout way that we should look for one. This means that, once again, we must read the clues *literally*. Suppose the compiler has this simple anagram:

> *Shrub* (anag.) (5)
> answer: *brush*

Instead of writing 'shrub, anag'. he might write 'shrub, pulled apart'. In other words, the actual constituent letters of s, h, r, u, b have been 'pulled apart' and then put together again in a different way. But that wouldn't be enough to form a complete clue; it is only a secondary clue.

We need a definition of the solution to complete it (in this case, 'brush'), so the whole thing might read:

> *Shrub pulled apart and made cleaner* (5)
> answer: *brush*

S–h–r–u–b has been pulled apart and remade into b–r–u–s–h – which is something that cleans. Note that all references to anagrams have gone, yet there is a distinct hint that there is one there.

> *Boots remade to give a fillip* (5)
> answer: *boost*

The definition here is 'to give a fillip' (i.e., boost); the secondary clue suggests that b–o–o–t–s can be 'remade', or reconstructed to make b–o–o–s–t.

> *Miser sped, tumbled, left his mark* (9)
> answer: *impressed*

'Tumbled' suggests that the letters m–i–s–e–r–s–p–e–d have been jumbled or tumbled about, into the order of i–m–p–r–e–s–s–e–d, which could mean 'left his mark'.

In the foregoing examples the anagram has been at the start of the clue, but there is no rule that this must be so. It might just as well be in the middle, or at the end. Nevertheless, wherever it is, somewhere in the complete clue we usually find a definition of the correct answer.

> *Removes the minced steak* (5)
> answer: *takes*

The definition is 'removes'='takes'. We arrive at this by 'mincing' the letters in s–t–e–a–k.

> *Small price for spilling cup on reef* (4,5)
> answer: *four pence*

Definition, 'small price', which aptly fits 4p. By 'spilling' the letters c–u–p–o–n–r–e–e–f we can make f–o–u–r–p–e–n–c–e.

There are occasions when words comprising an anagram are separated by a word, usually a preposition, which is *not* used in the anagram. For example:

> *Sidesman confused her with us* (5)
> answer: *usher*

The definition is 'sidesman'='usher'. An anagram is indicated by 'confused'. In this case the letters h–e–r are 'confused' with the letters u–s.

Now for a trickier example:

> *Single pin, when straightened, could turn a spool (8,5)*
> *answer: spinning-wheel*

The definition here is at the end; a spinning-wheel is something that can 'turn a spool'. The secondary clue, indicating an anagram, tells us that some words must be 'straightened' to form the answer. The catch is in the punctuation, inserted so that the whole sentence reads sensibly. Ignore the commas and 'straighten' the first *three* words, including 'when'. So:

> *s–i–n–g–l–e–p–i–n–w–h–e–n* makes *'spinning-wheel'*.

It ran about but it may stand at station

Now an example where the anagram comes in the middle of the clue:

> *To get proof, I confront Mai frenziedly (12)*
> *answer: confirmation*

'Proof'='confirmation'. To get it we need to put into a state of frenzy, the letters in 'I confront Mai'.

By now we will have realized that there are thousands of words in the English language which can be used to suggest anagrams, *provided they skilfully fit the context:* they must be in the appropriate metaphorical vein. To emphasize this, let us take another look at the above examples of disguised anagrams.

The miser who sped, and 'tumbled', made sense; but if it had been 'miser sped, minced' the effect would have been nonsensical. Again the 'minced' steak was a sensible suggestion of an anagram; a 'muddled' steak would have been rather silly. 'Spilling' a cup made sense; to suggest it should be 'straightened' would be stupid.

There follows a list of words of the type often used to disguise an anagram. We must remember, however, that there's no rule about this; it doesn't necessarily follow that the use of such words *must* indicate an anagram.

about	*in a frenzy*	*redisposed*
all over the place	*in a mess*	*reeling*
amok	*in a muddle*	*refashioned*
around	*in a stew*	*remoulded*
awkwardly	*in a whirl*	*reorganized*
awry	*in chaos*	*reset*
badly	*in disarray*	*ruined*
battered	*in disorder*	*run wild*
blown up	*in knots*	*scattered*
broken	*in pieces*	*scrambled*
buckling	*in ruins*	*set*
bust,-ed	*in smithereens*	*shakily*
caught up	*incoherent,-ly*	*smashed*
chaotic	*involved*	*somehow*
clumsy	*jumbled*	*somersaulting*
concealed	*knotted*	*sorted out*
confused	*made*	*spilt, spilling*
confusion	*made into, up*	*straightened*
contorted	*madly*	*strangely*
crooked-ly	*makes*	*stray,-ed,-ing*
crazy	*mashed*	*tangled*
curious,-ly	*messy*	*torn apart*
different	*minced*	*tossed*
disarranged	*mixed,-up*	*troubled*
displaced	*muddled*	*tumbled*
disposed	*needs remaking*	*turbulent*
distilled	*needs revision, etc.*	*twisted*
distorted	*odd,-ly*	*unknotted*
disturbed	*out*	*unscrambled*
drunk,-enly	*outcome of*	*untwisted*
exploding	*overturned*	*unwound*
erupting	*peculiar,-ly*	*upset*
extraordinary	*possible,-bly*	*variation*

frenzied	*produces*	*varied*
from	*product of*	*variety of*
gone adrift	*pulled apart*	*wandering*
gone haywire	*put in order*	*whirling*
gone mad, etc.	*queer,-ly*	*wild,-ly*
haphazard,-ly	*ragged,-ly*	*wrecked*
hashed	*rambling*	*wrong,-ly*
haywire	*rearrange,-d,-ment*	
hazy	*rebuilt*	

Now a few practical hints for resolving anagrams. As already suggested, Lexicon cards and Scrabble tiles can be helpful. A novice might find it useful to make a set of letters, drawing them on to pieces of card about three-quarters of an inch square. When these are haphazardly moved about into different positions an anagram sometimes almost 'solves itself'.

A scribbling pad helps. Letters written in a cluster are easier to arrange into a word than are those in a straight line; the eye sees possibilities more easily.

Another tip is to study the number of letters carefully. We might be staring glumly at a clue whose solution is shown by (5,6). Total, 11 letters. Are there one, two or three consecutive words in the clue whose letters together add up to 11? If yes, it's worth asking: Could they be an anagram?

With anagrams, usually the more letters there are in a word, the easier it is to solve. Long words are often an extension of short root words. They are apt to have similar group endings. Examples:

> -ious (*dubious, obnoxious*)
> -iously (*viciously, piously*)
> -ness (*fondness, greediness*)
> -fulness (*gratefulness, spitefulness*)
> -lessness (*carelessness, restlessness*)
> -ality, ility, bility (*joviality, instability*)
> -ance, ence (*maintenance, independence*)
> -ough, ought (*cough, thought*)

Frequent beginnings of words include con-, comm-,

dis-, indis-, uncomm-, uncon-. Other frequent endings include -able, -er, -ing, -ture, -ure. And so on.

If these combinations appear in an anagram it's worth lightly striking them out to see if an identifiable root word remains. Often it does. (When '-lessness' is struck out of an anagram there's not much left!) For example:

Bail pa in city (anag.) (*For drunkenness?*) (*12*)

It would be a fair guess that such a single word might end in '-ility', '-cility', '-ality' or '-bility'. If we experiment by striking these out we are eventually left with a–p–a–i–n–c. With the clue's hint of 'drunkenness' before us, it is a short step to solve 'incapability'. Or this:

Snug, these sloths! (anag.) (*No consideration!*) (*15*)

One word – and 's' appearing four times, 'e' twice, 'l' and 'n' once each! Surely this *must* end in 'lessness'? Knock that out and 'u–g–t–h–o–t–h' remains. From there it's but a short step to the solution, 'thoughtlessness'.

Test Word 3

(Solution on page 99)

This Test Word is designed for absolute beginners. Solvers with more experience of quick puzzles may prefer to pass immediately to the harder anagram puzzle on page 29.

Across

5 Delayed with tangled tale (4)
6 Boring instruments of muddled laws (4)
8 Add sound with new bud (3)
9 New tea to consume (3)
10 Extinction from hated crash (5)
12 Pointed weapon reaps afresh (5)
13 Oddly evens number (5)
14 Crazy feast results in exploits (5)
17 Voter upset sort of treasure (5)
19 Fashionable trams smashed (5)
20 Opt around for drug (3)

22 Lil is upset and sick (3)
23 Earth from silo mixture (4)
24 Node (anag.) (4)

Down

1 Bad arrangement for expert (3)
2 Outcast to repel in confusion (5)
3 Scattered straw makes skin blemishes (5)
4 Lea disturbed for drink (3)
5 Swelling from squashed plum (4)
7 Rescue a broken flower holder (4)
10 Valuable violin turned into board game (5)
11 Throbbing earth creates a beater (5)
15 Cupid is sore upset! (4)
16 Joyous look for miles around (5)
17 Badly rated commerce (5)
18 Live horribly, horrible (4)
21 Heavy weight not out (3)
22 Dark fluid excited kin (3)

Test Word 4

(Solution on page 100)

Across
1 I'm teen champ overthrown for arraignment (11)
6 Lear confused the nobleman (4)
7 Anatolian goat makes a wild groan agonizingly (6)
9 Lost, seen wandering without expression (8)
11 Led darts wildly to get astride (8)
13 Makes fast sale by arrangement (6)
14 Girl who has muddled visa? (4)
15 Enamel telly exploded by essentials (11)

Down
1 Incalculable effect of processing sable in time (11)
2 Mother pet ran amok (6)
3 Maths nun resolved for the game pursuer (8)
4 Hard black wood from chewed bone (4)
5 Hasty knell's wrong and getting no gratitude (11)
8 Try a felt alternative for the deflated tube (4,4)
10 Lad I've tormented into a hellish fiend (1,5)
12 Converted fuel up chimney (4)

Test Word 5 (Recap) (Solution on page 101)

Across

1 Glimpsed and ricochetted (7)
4 Agreements among Shop Act signatories (5)
7 Mixed nonet holds with mortise (5)
9 English river from Alps to Urals! (5)
10 Ted in a mission, scattering, scattering (13)
11 Swell out to speak at length (6)
12 Ordered GI, save face (6)
15 On appro, position Alec holds is being considered (13)
18 Put right in the beam ends (5)
19 Sorted mails for Mohammedan world (5)
20 Polishing powder used to make extreme rybat (5)
21 Being wanted, resided all over the place (7)

Down

1 Curfewed, with narrow entrance outside (5)
2 Try nice cone of assorted sweets (13)
3 Extract essence from Di's tilth (6)
4 I bit lip as Boer renewed some likely chances (13)
5 Welsh dog motor scooter (5)
6 Hush gag (7)
8 Lana's tweaking of the nose (5)

11 Reduce exhaust (7)
13 Quash something in Mann, ultra-humanist (5)
14 Caught scent, knocked breathless (6)
16 Harangue from pastor at ease (5)
17 Crooked medal for crippled (5)

5

Words Within Words

Countless English words can be broken down into two or more smaller words, or into recognized abbreviations for other words, or into a combination of both. This useful fact is exploited to the full by compilers of cryptic puzzles.

It is essential that we, as solvers, should understand the technique of breaking down words and building them up again. In this chapter we will confine ourselves to the simplest kind of 'words within words', leaving abbreviations and other symbols until later.

One important aspect of this type of clue must never be overlooked. That is, when we have broken down a word into syllables which themselves make short words, *these individually will have probably little or no relation to the meaning of the word as a whole*.

For example, 'contrite', meaning penitent, may be split up into 'con' (to study or scan closely) and 'trite' (meaning hackneyed). When isolated, neither of these constituents has any connection with 'penitent'.

Then 'penitent' itself may be divided into three small words with unrelated meanings, e.g., 'pen', 'I', and 'tent'.

On the other hand there are words which *partly* form another word while the remaining letters, on their own, are largely meaningless. 'Trombone' gives us 'trom', which is not a word, and 'bone', which is. 'Spasmodic' starts with the word 'spas' or spasm – but 'modic' is not a word.

When a compiler breaks down a word in this way, he usually gives a secondary clue to the little word as well as a definitive clue to the complete one. Furthermore, he will probably indicate whether the secondary word is at the beginning, the middle or the end of the complete answer.

> *A fool starts to attack* (6)
> answer: assail

'Ass' (who often equals a fool in crossword puzzles) *starts* the word 'assail'.

> *Mournful procession but starts off with amusement* (7)
> answer: funeral

'Fun', or amusement, starts it off.

> *Move first with this bird* (10)
> answer: budgerigar

A more difficult one, this. But re-read the clue as 'With this bird "move" comes first', and we see where 'budge' fits in.

In every one of the above examples the compiler has told us how to *start* the answer. If the inner word were to be found at *the end*, he might give us clues like this:

> *A sticky end for this princess!* (5)
> answer: begum (be-gum)
> *Of local government a friend at last* (9)
> answer: municipal (munici-pal)

Overland carrier that's four-fifths water

When the secondary word forms a major part of the total word (i.e., in its number of letters) the compiler may hint as much, or even say so outright. For example,

> *To search a suspect is mainly a hazard* (5)
> answer: frisk

'Frisk' is *mainly* made up of r–i–s–k

> *Peculiar, it's mostly mountains!* (7)
>
> *answer: strange*

'Strange' is *mostly* made up of r–a–n–g–e.

If the smaller word falls somewhere inside the larger one, it may be described as being 'taken in by', or 'forming part of' the large one. Or the major word may be said to have 'swallowed' another, or to be 'gripping it', to 'comprise' or 'enclose' or 'enfold' it, and so on. Here are some examples:

> '*rib*' forms part of '*tribe*'
>
> '*Paleface*' may have swallowed '*ale*'
>
> '*cove*' can be involved in '*discovery*'
>
> '*shoddily*' carries a '*hod*'
>
> '*cartoon*' uses '*art*'
>
> '*ant*' is in the '*pantry*'

Again, the compiler will select the metaphor or figure of speech which is most suitable for the complete phrase.

> *Maths honours holder has swallowed fish* (8)
>
> *answer: wrangler*

The Cambridge 'wrangler' has *swallowed* 'angle', i.e., 'fish'. (Note the catch here; 'fish' has been used as a verb, not as a noun, in the clue.)

Now we turn to words made up of two or more smaller words which again are totally unrelated to each other in meaning. For example:

Office	=	*off*+*ice*
shindig	=	*shin*+*dig*
prodigal	=	*prod*+*I*+*gal*
enterprise	=	*enter*+*prise*
scarlet	=	*scar*+*let*
martingale	=	*mar*+*tin*+*gale*
		or *mart*+*in*+*gale*
		or *mar*+*ting*+*ale*
		or *martin*+*gale*

It doesn't take much imagination to see to what tricks a compiler may resort when he starts splitting a word up into pieces in this way. There is one unwritten rule that all compilers observe meticulously whenever they have chopped up a word. *Their clue will always give an accurate indication of the order in which the pieces of word appear.* A clue to 'martingale' would not read in such a way that it could apply to 'tin–gale–mar' or to 'gale–mar–tin'.

Obviously words within words are nearly always very short, and puzzle solvers soon train themselves to think in brief terms. We have to find short synonyms for long words, not to mention abbreviations (dealt with in the next chapter).

'Ma' and 'pa' are always turning up in puzzles, being handy versions of mother, father and parent. 'Red' (for Communist, revolutionary, or Russian) is always with us. We soon learn that 'tan' may mean a colour or to give a beating or thrashing. A 'fellow' may be 'man', or 'don' (university), or possibly a boy's short name like Ron, Ted, or Eric, three regular favourites! There are scores of examples in the glossary at the end of this book – and the hard-driven compilers are for ever trying to think up new and original ones.

The simplest clue to a composite word is where the smaller words are dealt with in their correct sequence. If we take 'pattern' as an example: 'pat' may be said to *take*, or *come to*, or *get*, or *be followed* by, 'tern'. The compiler will find two synonyms for these little words; he may well choose 'an Irishman' for 'Pat', and 'the bird' for 'tern'. So:

> *Model Irishman gets the bird* (7)
> *answer: pattern*

'Model' is the definition of 'pattern'. Secondary clue? Pat gets the tern!

To make it a little less obvious, the clue might be:

> *Model girl takes a bird* (7)

'Pat' has now become a girl's name, which broadens the field considerably (though 'model' should put us quickly on the road to 'pattern' – while 'tern', like the 'emu', is another bird who frequents the pages of the compiler's notebook).

Or, to make it harder still:

> *Irishman joins a winger for example* (7)

Though 'Pat' has become more obvious again, the 'winger', or one that uses wings, or flier, or bird, is a somewhat obscure clue for 'tern'. But now we have 'example', as a definitive clue for 'pattern', to simplify things again.

Here are some more straightforward examples:

> *Wise counsellor for chaps coming to hill* (6)
> *answer: mentor*

(i.e., 'men' *coming to* 'tor' = 'wise counsellor')

> *Rust seen after mist creates doubt* (8)
> *answer: mistrust*

(i.e., after 'mist' we see 'rust' = 'doubt'. Here both halves of the solution were printed in the clue, yet because they had been switched they were not immediately obvious)

This method can be carried a stage further.

Take 'debated', whose letters can be broken down to de–bat–ed. Here we see the word 'bat' *inside* the word 'deed'; or, as the compiler might put it, 'a striker caught in the act' (i.e., a 'bat' – striker of ball – *caught inside* a 'deed').

We are going to find a lot of clues of this type in cryptic puzzles. We must watch out for clues telling us that something 'goes round' something else, or 'takes in' something. Similar hints: 'envelops', 'encircled', 'within', 'imprisoned' – in fact, any metaphor which suggests that a group of letters is enclosed within another one, e.g.:

> *Torturer traps men between hills* (9)
> *answer: tormentor*

(i.e., 'torturer' made up of 'men' between 'tor' and 'tor', or two hills.)

> *Eastern Temple Father brought in a god* (6)
> *answer: pagoda*

(i.e., 'pa' has 'a god' brought into it; p–agod–a)

> *Delight of fields in clean environment* (8)
> *answer: pleasure*

(i.e., delight, or pleasure, made up of 'leas' (fields) in 'pure' (clean) environment: p–leas–ure)

We must also watch out for a part of some extraneous word appearing in the solution, usually indicated by such words or phrases as 'some', 'part of', 'a bit', etc. For example:

> *Musical instrument to prohibit with some joy* (5)
> *answer: banjo*

(i.e., 'ban', or prohibit, is seen with only 'jo', or *some* 'joy').

Thus a parson might be said to conclude with 'a lot of song' (son); or a lesson could be said to open with 'some smiles' or 'half smiles' (les).

In the next Test Word all the solutions contain other, usually unrelated, words, with the exception of one anagram.

Test Word 6

(Solution on page 102)

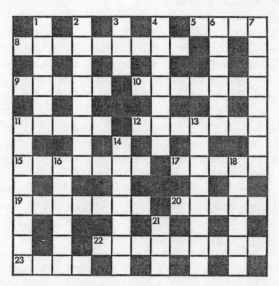

Across

5 Pleasure ground largely a floating menagerie (4)
8 In a low state; press is there! (9)
9 Rid heart of haughtiness (5)
10 Reverse with ship's record makes work pile-up (7)
11 Pastor's congregation mostly shut up (5)
12 Fast mover, nearly all hurry! (7)
15 Aries takes poles for gun-barrel cleaners (7)
17 I, with some gloom, make snow hut (5)
19 General pardon: am taking bird home with letter (7)
20 Chose Ted for the major part (5)
22 Unseemly conduct taking in stage scenery (9)
23 Gape, absorbing bit of chaff (4)

Down

1 Pet, start rolling, for driving spirit (6)
2 Film controller is half Italian dictator! (8)
3 As softly come together as a snake (3)

4 Makes off secretly, having swallowed Cambridge water (7)
6 Sauntered, much blood lost (6)
7 Australian jumper has eaten garfish (8)
11 Class comes to join together with ceremony (8)
13 Poe's gong (anag.) used for breakfast? (3,5)
14 Preparing for printer, takes in tin (7)
16 Tiny fish with present ending (6)
18 Undo the doors, a writer's within (4,2)
21 He begins to cut down (3)

6

Anagrams Within Words

When we were looking at anagrams, and later at 'words within words', we omitted one ploy which bridges the two forms of clue. That is the use of *mixed* words, or anagrams, 'within' words.

Let us first recap our analysis of the last group of 'words within words' in chapter five. Here we saw that one complete word can be 'held', or 'captured', or be 'within', or be 'taken in by' another word. Alternatively, the latter or outer word may be said to 'surround', or 'grip', or 'embrace' or 'take in' the inner word, and so on. To recap further, take two of the last batch of examples,

> *Eastern Temple Father takes in an idol* (6)
> *answer:* pagoda p(a–god)a
> *Delight of fields in unsoiled surroundings* (8)
> *answer:* pleasure p(leas)ure

Now if the compiler wanted to make us work twice as hard he might decide to offer us *half* of the answer in the form of an anagram. So the first example might become

> *Eastern Temple Father takes in a wandering dog* (6)
> *answer:* p(a–g–o–d)a

because here 'a god' has become 'a dog' *wandering*, or an anagram (both 'taken in' by pa, or father, of course). The second example might become

> *Delight of mixed drinks in unsoiled surroundings (8)*
> answer: p(l–e–a–s)ure

because 'leas' = mixed-up 'ales', or drinks.

So when we read such clues we must identify *two* signs: one, that part of the complete word is an 'inner' word, and two, that something is 'mixed-up' or 'wandering', i.e., an anagram. In cryptic puzzles we find this kind of clue usually appears in a fairly easily identifiable form. Once we are used to seeing anagrams and 'words within words' we soon recognize any merging of the two. Where they appear in these Test Words they should be fairly easy to solve.

However, it is a development of this type of clue (by the use of more obscure words and abstract allusions) that is often found in those really difficult puzzles which can keep scholars occupied for hours, or even days. Although those are beyond the scope of this book it is as well to understand their basic principles. A few more examples:

> *Pant round untidy den with a hanger-on (7)*
> answer: pendant

i.e. 'pant *round* 'end' (untidy 'den'), for p–end–ant

> *Shortened awkward grid in a cot (8)*
> answer: abridged

i.e., 'grid' awkwardly can be 'ridg'. Put it in 'a bed' (a cot) to give 'a–b(ridg)ed', or shortened.

> *Sam, trapped in wild furze, is pretty flimsy material (8)*
> answer: gossamer

i.e., 'Sam', trapped or held in *wild* 'gorse' (or furze) becomes 'gos(Sam)er,' or a pretty flimsy material.

The last example is tricky, because the solver's first reaction would be to treat 'furze' as the *wild* anagram, instead of first translating it into 'gorse'.

The next Test Word comprises solely such clues. A hint: some of its anagrams are *stated* (such as 'pant', 'grid' and 'Sam' in the above examples) while others must first be converted (such as 'bed', 'sailor' and 'furze' in the same set of examples).

Test Word 7

(Solution on page 103)

Across

1 With variations Pat starts to record (4)
3 Greek city hides trap set another way (6)
7 Oar broken and split in round of duty (4)
8 Engines have internal Toro components (6)
10 Protector is broken reed first and last (8)
13 Religious garment with crooked stem in air-hole (8)
16 Mock terribly dreadful heart (6)
17 Jagged Alp makes most of tropical tree (4)
18 Jumbled rot ending extract (6)
19 Average man mostly (4)

Down

1 Harangue concludes with crazy dare (6)
2 Partly pout about; wholly postponed (3,3)
4 Confused effort winds up estate (8)
5 In twisted tor I disturb peace (4)
6 Angry asp dominates church recess (4)
9 Produce a mixed green with broken finish (8)
11 Discuss new label engulfed by river (6)
12 Flower part finished with poor name (6)
14 Unemployed start off with wry cover (4)
15 Upset ref makes lot of worry (4)

7

Abbreviations and Contractions

Abbreviations might be described as the red corpuscles in a puzzle's lifeblood; without them some would look rather anaemic. We saw a few pale examples of this in recent Test Words, where some of the clues might have been enlivened had we then been able to use abbreviations.

In the last chapter we considered complete words found inside larger ones. Now we will see how acceptable abbreviations may also be manipulated as components of words. In fact, from now on we should train ourselves to become thoroughly abbreviation conscious.

Incidentally, the solutions themselves are rarely found in the form of abbreviations. If, on occasion, something like 'RSVP' or 'OHMS' is a correct solution, then the clue ends with (abbrev.) (1,1,1,1) – which is rather a give-away! So a compiler will only resort to it if it is unavoidable for 'holding', or locking with, letters of an important solution for which he has been inspired to write a brilliant clue.

In crossword puzzles, abbreviations are nearly always limited to those found listed at the end of the average standard dictionary or in everyday reference books. Their clues fall into two categories:

1. Straightforward definitions to recognized abbreviations, which are comparatively easy to solve.

2. Allusive definitions, which involve two mental steps to get the answer.

To illustrate the difference between the two, let us suppose a clue includes 'able-bodied seaman'. We might presume that this meant 'AB' in the answer. Indeed, if 'able-bodied' appeared alone, we would probably transcribe it as 'AB'. This is a first-category example.

But suppose the clue made reference to a 'deckhand', or a 'tar', or possibly to 'Jack', we would have to take two steps. The first would translate the reference into 'seaman' and the second would translate seaman into 'AB'.

If this second category sounds involved we can soon be reassured. The conventions of the crossword language are easily learned, easily discovered, and easily remembered. Here are just a few examples of straightforward abbreviations with which we are most familiar, and which turn up again and again:

ac or acc	*accounts*	RA	*Royal Academician*
BA	*Bachelor of Arts*		*Royal Artillery*
Dr	*debtor, doctor*	rd	*road*
f ff	*forte* (*musically loud*)	RE	*Royal Engineers*
hr	*hour*	ry	*railway*
L	*left, Liberal*	st	*Saint, street*
MA	*Master of Arts*	TT	*teetotaller*

The points of the compass, for example, can be abbreviated to 'N', 'S', 'E', and 'W'. So if a clue referred to a 'compass point' we would immediately think of one of these letters. But an allusive definition would be less obvious, perhaps referring only to 'a point', or to a 'direction'. Another variation is the introduction of North and South Poles, which may simply turn up as 'poles'. Well, we all know there are all sorts of poles; they may live in Poland, or be flagstaffs, or be bracketed with rods and perches – but in a crossword they might well be our old friends 'n' and 's'.

Or let us have a quick look at the letter 'O'. There are many ways of indicating it – by 'zero', perhaps, or 'nothing', or 'nil'; possibly a 'ring', or 'circle'; maybe even a 'duck' (as in cricket). All useful words for weaving into clues.

Earlier in this chapter we looked at a short list of abbreviations with 'straightforward' definitions. Suppose we examine the same list again, but with the allusive definitions a compiler might use. (The use of 'little' or 'small' often indicates the presence of an abbreviation.)

ac or acc	*bill*
BA	*graduate; scholar; man with degree; learned person*

Dr   *medical man; medico; medical practitioner; doctor; doc*

ff   *loud; very loud; loudly; strongly*

hr   *hour; a period; some time*

L   *Left; to port; a pound (£); a learner; Liberal; one*

MA   *as BA*

MD   *as Dr*

RA   *artist; famous artist; painter; man of art; brushworker; the gunners*

rd   *road; small road; little road; way; route; thoroughfare*

RE   *the engineers; sappers*

ry   *railway; lines; transport system*

st   *saint; holy man; good man; good person; street; little street; small street; route; thoroughfare; station*

TT   *teetotaller; abstainer; man of no spirit; non-drinker*

Now for some examples of abbreviations forming part of the solution. While we still expect the clue to contain a definition of the complete answer our secondary clues should lead us to its component abbreviations.

> *Fanatical artist takes offer* (5)
> *answer: rabid*

i.e., 'RA' (artist)+'bid' (offer) makes 'rabid', or fanatical.

> *Doctor and a scholar produce play* (5)
> *answer:drama*

'Dr' (doctor)+'a' 'MA' (a scholar) produce 'drama', or play. (Note how the indefinite article 'a' forms part of the answer. We must always be alert for any word or letter being used in this way.)

> *British Rail owning a poet* (8)
> *answer: Browning*

i.e., 'BR' (British Rail)+'owning' makes poet Browning. A less obvious version of the same clue might read:

> *Railway network possessing a linesman* (8)
> *answer: Browning*

'BR (railway network)+'owning' (possessing) makes Browning. Here the word 'linesman' could have put us off the scent, for he is not somebody to do with railway lines but one who *writes* 'lines', i.e. a poet. The word falls into the same category of less-usual meanings as those discussed in the chapter on multiple definitions (including 'butter', 'bloomer', 'flower', etc.).

The diminutive plays an important part in the world of crosswords. It is often applied to the names of people. 'Little Diana' becomes 'Di' and 'young Sidney' is reduced to 'Sid': this precocious pair are apt to pop up all over the place. We soon become familiar, too, with 'small Desmond' ('Des'), 'little Violet' (Vi'), 'young Robert' ('Bob') and so on. 'Young Edward' may appear as 'Ted', 'Ed', or even 'Eddie'.

Incidentally, we must keep a permanent eye on public figures! Some personalities in the news may have names which can be shortened easily; some also have convenient synonyms. Mr Edward Heath provides a typical example. When he headed the government the 'prime minister' in a clue often turned out to be 'Ed' or 'Ted', while 'Heath', of course, also lends scope for variations! We should keep an eye on actors, writers, heroes (and villains), and such idols as cricketers, footballers and tennis players. Sportsmen, past and present, with names like Grace, Best, Moore, and Snow will inevitably flit among the clues from time to time.

> *Little Diana comes to emphasize misfortune* (8)
> *answer: distress*

i.e., 'Di' *comes to* 'stress'=Di–stress (misfortune). Alternatively

> *Wretched state of little Diana's lock of hair* (8)
> *answer: distress*

i.e., Wretched state=distress, *made up of* 'Di's tress', or lock of hair.

> *Sledge from young Robert's Lancashire town* (9)
> *answer: bobsleigh*

i.e., sledge=bobsleigh – *from* Bob's Leigh.

Contractions may also apply to all sorts of nouns. Where there are recognized abbreviations, useful hints like 'little', 'small', 'short' help to draw our attention to them.

'A little time' may mean a shortened spelling of year, hour, minute or second, which respectively become 'yr', 'hr', 'min' and 'sec'. A 'small mountain' might simply mean the abbreviation 'mt'. A small 'weight' could indicate 'oz' (conversely a 'big weight' usually refers to 'ton'). But the same abbreviations can also be used *without* the 'small'.

After a brief time the Yorkshire river is safe (6)
answer: secure

i.e., 'brief time' = sec (abbreviation of 'second'). Yorkshire River = Ure. 'Ure *after* 'sec' = sec–Ure, or safe.

String of wagons Tuesday? Right! First class to the North

We must also remember that articles and prepositions such as 'an' and 'in' and 'the' may be part of the solution. Thus:

Sailors in the drink! (8)
answer: absinthe

i.e., ABs (sailors) + 'in' + 'the' making 'absinthe', a drink. Sometimes we may find it necessary to translate phrases as well as words into one-, two-, or three-letter substitutes.

Suppose we read that something 'is in order', or is 'approved of', or is 'acceptable'; we might convert it, in the first stage, to 'all right', and then reduce that phrase to 'OK'.

In some puzzles slang may be banned altogether. In others it may be used with such qualifications as 'vulgarly' or 'commonly speaking', or 'slang' may be added, to indicate that though such an expression may be in general use we look down our noses at it. For example, 'it's commonly all right' puts 'OK' firmly in its place!

A reference to a 'stunning blow' or 'getting floored' might lead us to a 'knock-out', which in turn could be reduced to 'KO'. If something is 'socially acceptable' or 'upper class' it might be reduced, in the current idiom, to a simple 'U' (or conversely, 'non-U', as the case might be).

Things 'outsize' can be cut down to 'OS'. A 'motorway' may come down to 'M'. A 'beginner', 'novice', 'tyro' or 'apprentice' may all indicate a 'Learner', which in turn is symbolized simply by 'L'.

> *Outsize plunder for big rare bird* (6)
> *answer: osprey*

i.e., OS+prey=osprey, a rare, large bird.

The musical scale provides many useful abbreviations. 'A note' might indicate any of the letters (in music) A, B, C, D, E, F, G. Or it might refer to the notes of the tonic sol-fa, i.e., 'do' or 'doh', 're' or 'ra', 'mi', 'fa' or 'fah', 'so', 'la', 'si' or 'te'.

> *Southern motorway's all right, note the fire signal* (5)
> *answer: smoke*

i.e., S–M–OK–e, or sign of fire.

> *Note to two learners: it's a grinder!* (4)
> *answer: mill*

i.e., 'mi'=musical note, *to*, or added on to, two Ls (abbreviations for learners)=mi–LL, a machine for grinding.

Take divisions of time. 'The morning', or 'before noon', would almost certainly be represented by a.m., the 'afternoon' by p.m., 'the day before' by 'eve'. While 'a short time' might be 'min', 'sec' or 'tick', a 'long time' could be 'age', 'era' or 'eon'. Whole eras may be indicated by BC or AD. In between come 'hr', 'wk', and 'mon'. Of course the names of months may be cut down to 'Jan', 'Feb', 'Mar', etc., and weekdays to 'Mon', 'Tues', 'Wed', etc., or even to 'M', 'Tu', 'W', 'Th', 'F', 'S'.

> *A wee drop for the doctor before noon (4)*
> answer: *dram*

i.e., Doctor=dr, before noon=a.m. so dr–am.

Other abbreviations in frequent use include 'op' (for 'opus' or 'work'); 'RN' (Royal Navy); 'ac' or 'acc' (for account or bill); 'CA' (chartered accountant); 'ious' (debts, or I–owe–yous), a very useful one, this, considering how many words end in 'ious'.

If somebody in a clue is said to act 'with hesitation' it may well indicate '–er'; in the same vein 'with uncertainty' might be '–um'. (I must admit to a strong personal dislike of 'er' and 'um'.)

> *I show uncertainty after work making drug (5)*
> answer: *opium*

i.e., 'I'+'um' *after* 'op' – making opium, or drug.

> *Inquisitive beast has debts (7)*
> answer: *curious*

i.e., 'cur', or beast+ 'ious', or debts, making 'curious' or inquisitive.

Nobody can accuse crossword compilers of insularity. They rope in people from other countries and toss off references to their rivers and towns, their currencies and their languages. We will become accustomed to references to 'the French' and 'the German' in clues, when invariably literal translations are required. 'The', in French, may be 'le', 'la' or 'les'. Similarly, 'the German', 'the Spanish', 'the Italian' may simply mean 'der', 'el' and 'il'. Likewise '*of* the French' would probably mean 'de la', 'du' or 'des', etc.

The initial letter of a word might be referred to as its 'leader' or 'head', e.g., 'army's leader' could be 'a'. Similarly, the last letter could be its 'tail' or 'end'.

> *State of the French merchandise (8)*
> answer: *Delaware*

i.e., Delaware is one of the United States. Constructed by 'de la' ('of the' in French)+'ware' meaning merchandise.

A knowledge of *all* the US states, and their abbreviations, can be helpful, as 'state' is a recurring word in clues.

A Frenchman, of course, is just 'M'; a 'German house-wife' invariably 'frau'. But we must look for subtler allusions, too. 'A Parisian leavetaking' might be merely 'adieu', or 'gratitude in France' could be reduced to 'merci'. Other examples: 'an Italian waterway' (Po); 'German aristocrat' (graf); 'Russian' (Red).

Many abbreviations and shortened words which appear frequently in crossword puzzles are listed in our glossary. However, it must be emphasized again that they are only there as likely or *possible* interpretations in clues.

In the next Test Word all the clues except one use abbreviations or contractions. The exception is a straight-forward anagram. (Before tackling the Test Word it might be a good idea to browse through the glossary to get the feel of some of the abbreviations in frequent use.) For those who might get stuck, it should not be necessary to peep at the solution; if help is needed, the glossary should give enough to get the Test Word completed.

Test Word 8 (Solution on page 103)

Across

7 Harshly criticize a little mother for American republic (6)

8 Uproar when not in credit with Yard's leader (6)

9 All done, company member taking the French to Ted (9)

10 Consumed a note (3)

12 Takes off small saint; rest in peace with old Bob! (6)

14 Harken aboard big cutters (6)

15 Gunners taking the radius? Yes, indeed! (6)

17 Cora tripped to opposite poles for some oak seeds (6)

18 Nothing to the theologian is strange (3)

19 Announce publicly muddling is averted (9)

22 Give me Rhode Island number for a kind of wool (6)

23 Ass of a fellow with winding device (6)

Down

1 South European ditto, taking in silver (4)
2 Artificial illumination having left, am with dilemma (9)
3 A loving touch brings care to the ship (6)
4 Between Post Office and Royal Society we make strong nations (6)
5 Little way with yak's head for hog's home (3)
6 Brothers! Train network takes direction, then goes round the King! (8)
11 Rebelling about electric unit in gravity (9)
13 Airline, taking Divine to the French King, comes to senseless talker (8)
16 Fiery revolutionary takes nothing in high tension (3-3)
17 Puts matters right as morning finishes (6)
20 She would shortly cast off (4)
21 US soldier goes to North for spirit (3)

8

Numbers

Another much-used form of abbreviation relates to numbers. As a group numbers appear in clues more frequently than other abbreviations and contractions, and individually they are represented in various ways – by letters, by Roman figures, and by colloquial terms. We may find 'o' suggested by 'zero', 'nothing', 'nil', 'circle', 'ring', or 'duck', among others. For example:

> *Went on horseback to ring for cattle round-up* (5)
> *answer: rodeo*

i.e., 'rode' *to* 'o'. Thus rodeo, or cattle round-up.

The word 'one' in a clue might appear in the answer as the singular indefinite clue 'a' or 'an', or by the 'i' or 'I' used in numerology. Example:

> *Sacked Fred gets round one* (5)
> *answer: fired*

i.e., 'Fred' *gets round* 'i', making F(i)red, or sacked.

A reference to 'two' in a clue might work both ways. It could indicate 'pr', short for 'pair', in the answer. Or 'two', 'twice', 'a couple' could be interpreted literally as showing that part of the answer appeared twice over. 'Isis' becomes 'is' *twice*. 'Pom-pom' is *a pair of* 'poms'. Example:

> *With a couple of tins make a boisterous dance* (6)
> *answer: cancan*

i.e., two 'cans'.

'Three' in a clue usually means what it says (unless a possible anagram of 'ether' or 'there') and probably refers to a trio of Graces, Musketeers or other identifiable people or objects. So 'three points' could be three of the four compass points N, S, E or W.

'Four', 'five' and 'six' are easily translated by roman

numerals into 'iv', 'v', and 'vi' respectively. Or they may be referred to euphemistically as 'teatime', 'afternoon' or 'early evening' . . . e.g., 'pivot' might become 'pot' *about* 'teatime' (p(iv)ot). Or, like the trio, the numbers could refer to well-known quartets, quintets and sextets. 'Six' or 'vi' may also be indicated by 'half a dozen'.

> *Rendered to general, having taken in four* (5)
> answer: *given*

i.e., 'rendered to' is a definition of 'given'. 'Gen' (short for 'general'), has *taken in* 'iv', thus: g(iv)en.

> *Confidential couple ate about teatime* (7)
> answer: *private*

i.e., 'confidential' is a definition of 'private'. 'Pr' is a little form of 'pair' or couple; 'iv' represents 'teatime'. Pr+ate *around* 'iv' make private, thus: pr(iv)ate.

'Nine' often works out as 'ix', as in:

> *Attach a couple of notes before nine* (5)
> answer: *affix*

i.e., 'Attach'='affix' made from 'a'+two 'ff's (musical notes) before 'ix'. Thus: a–ff–ix.

'Ten' in a clue often indicates 'x' in the answer, but sometimes it is to be taken literally as 't–e–n', as in a hidden word clue. 'Half a score' may also indicate 'ten' or 'x'.

> *Foreign Office with ten men in pink chase him* (3)
> answer: *fox*

i.e., 'F.O.' *with* 'x' makes fo-x. Definitive clue: 'Men in pink (huntsmen), chase him.' The trick here is to place an imaginary comma after 'ten'.

> *Dishevelled Mars wants ten to spruce up* (7)
> answer: *smarten*

i.e., *Dishevelled* 'Mars' (anag.)='smar'. *Wants* 'ten' to make 'smar–ten', or spruce up.

'Eleven' may indicate 'xi', of course. In a certain type of clue it might also indicate 'll'. 'Eleven' might also indicate a 'team' or 'side' (football, cricket, etc.).

> *Small thanks to team for getting a cab* (4)
> answer: *taxi*

i.e., 'ta'=abbreviated 'thank you'. Added to 'xi', or team, *gets* a cab, or ta–xi.

'Twelve' may be abbreviated to 'doz'; 'twenty', as we

have seen, may be shortened to 'score'.

Larger numbers are often reduced to 'L' (fifty); 'C' (a hundred); 'D' (five hundred); 'M' (a thousand). These numbers may also be referred to in vaguer terms, such as 'several', 'many', 'crowds of', 'large numbers', as appropriate. The word 'number', is often abbreviated to 'no'.

In cryptic puzzles we will naturally expect to find allusions to numbers in recognized groups, such as Three Graces, Nine Muses, Ten Commandments, Naughty Nineties, Roaring Forties, and so on.

All but four of the clues in the next Test Word have some connection with numbers.

Test Word 9 (Solution on page 104)

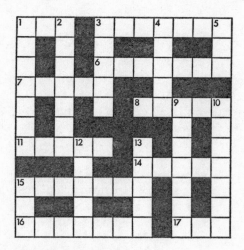

Across

1 A hundred note to one (3)
3 Confidential prattle about teatime (7)
6 Fifty to each six makes most of going (7)
7 Girl with nothing makes rope noose (5)
8 Take responsibility for a crowd to choose (5)
11 A thousand two hundred point madly to Islamic city (5)
14 She takes fifty-one North with 500-note (5)

15   Four in test of little importance (7)
16   Other CO ordered something to smoke (7)
17   Look at bishop's office (3)

Down

1   Applause, starting with a couple of hundred, ends with a thousand (7)
2   Flexible point to last one century (7)
3   Ten make an end of the garden bloomer (5)
4   Brilliant six, six died (5)
5   Work unit baffled Reg (3)
9   No mountains for fruit (7)
10   After ten, skilful can be held (7)
12   Hundred done with lid (5)
13   Apportion a 50-lot (5)
15   Short time in charge of twitch (3)

Test Word 10 (Recap)   (Solution on page 105)

Across

1   Troubled ways harder under century of fighting (7,5,3)
7   Bloomer in pa's territory (5)
8   In five hundred and one a far country (5)
10   Holy woman who might have dark habits (3)
11   King encircled by fragments breaks through (7)
13   Fuss from year zero (3)
14   Utterly exhausted, everyone included (3,2)
15   Tyrant upset poor about printing machine (9)
16   Skull bone fractured, I clip coat (9)
18   Glorify the good queen who's eaten pound! (5)
20   Mixed help for Welshman (3)
21   Fermented milk product of Thug Roy (7)
23   His kid hides mountain slipper (3)
24   Go aboard to make progress (3,2)
26   US soldier takes awkward spy for Romany (5)
28   When it is wise to shop before lunch (5,7,3)

Down

1   Avoiding hot game madly enjoying oneself (6,1,4,4)
2   A groove, in truth (3)

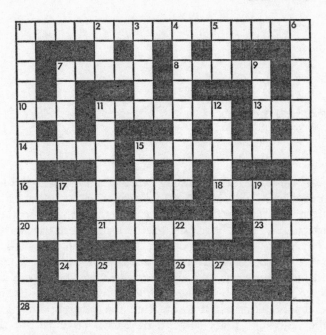

3 Lament for German capital in dire surroundings (5)
4 Odd spice and precious stone of bishops (9)
5 Free from pride (3)
6 How to go backwards (15)
7 Cancel what Ann ultimately holds (5)
9 Accumulate a large lump (5)
11 Brilliant array of Arcadian god making appeal to work (7)
12 Effervescent powder from medicinal plant in set (7)
15 Eight-sided coal got an order (9)
17 Lots of fish stick together (5)
19 Attempt a literary composition (5)
23 In a splurge Sam eggs on (5)
25 Make an effort to irritate (3)
27 Quietly I take pole to fix (3)

9

Acrobatics

So far we have dealt mainly with whole-word syllables, abbreviations and numbers following each other in a straight line. That is, the clues have presented word sections consecutively, usually relying on the formula that so-and-so 'takes', 'gets', 'meets', 'precedes', 'follows' such and such.

We broke away from this a little in the sections on words, abbreviations and numbers *within* words, but we are now going to see how the compiler can brighten up his clues by breaking right away from the 'straight line' and further mixing up its constituent parts. To illustrate the development it may be necessary to go over a little of the old ground first, but only briefly.

As a first example, we will take the word 'straying'. A conventional, straight-line clue of syllables and abbreviations might produce:

Wandering holy man with shaft of light takes note (8)

The solution is broken up like this: st–ray–in–g. Meaning 'wandering'.

Agreed, this is a cumbersome and dreary piece of work. But could s–t–r–a–y–i–n–g have been broken up differently? Certainly yes. So let us look at some alternatives.

First we might separate the single letter 'r' (short for 'right', 'rex', 'regina') as being enclosed by 'staying', thus:

st–(r)–aying

Or we might see 'ay' (meaning 'aye', or 'yes') enclosed by 'string', thus:

str–(ay)–ing

Or 'tr' (an abbreviation for 'trustee') enclosed by 'saying', thus:

s–(tr)–aying

Or 'ray' (fish, shaft of light, boy's name, snake, etc.) enclosed by 'sting', thus:

> st–(ray)–ing

Or 'tray' (e.g., a 'salver') enclosed by 'sing', thus:

> s–(tray)–ing

Or we might abandon the order of letters, knotting the word up further by breaking it down into 't' (an abbreviation for 'time') and an anagram, thus:

> T+syringa

Or make anagrams of two words, 'gray' (alternative spelling of 'grey') and 'tins', thus:

> gray+tins

Or extract 'RA' (artist or Royal Artillery or gunners) from an anagram of 'stingy', thus:

> stingy+RA

Or remove 'train', leaving ourselves with Sy (abbreviation for 'Surrey') and 'g' (musical note) thus:

> train+Sy+g

This list will do to be going on with, although it by no means exhausts all the possibilities. But it does illustrate the new scope which is opened up for the compiler.

Let us see how clues might be built round some of these new alternatives, remembering that each must still give a definition of 'straying'.

> *Right in staying, yet off course*
> answer: *straying*

or, to use the same idea less obviously

> *Right in remaining, yet off course*
> answer: *st–r–aying*
> *Off course? Yes, in file*
> answer: *str–ay–ing*

i.e., 'ay', or 'yes', in 'string' which here is used in the sense of a procession of people, etc., *not* a cord.

> *In speaking, short Trustee is getting lost*
> answer: *s–Tr–aying*

Here the 'short' Trustee is telling us to use the abbreviation 'Tr', inserted *into* 'saying'.

> *Cheat traps young Raymond into leaving straight and narrow*
> answer: *st–Ray–ing*

Note here that 'cheat', which looks like a noun, is really the verb to cheat, or 'to sting', in colloquial parlance. 'Ray' is trapped in 'sting', thus leaving the straight and narrow path.

> *Wandering chant about a salver*
> *answer: s–tray–ing*

Wandering, or straying, made from 'sing' about a 'tray'.

> *Getting lost rattling gray tins*

'Rattling' indicates the anagram of 'gray tins'.

> *Stingy artist crazily wandering*
> *answer: st–RA–ying*

'Crazily' suggests an anagram. It is made up of 'stingy' plus 'RA' (artist), to make straying or wandering.

> *Runaway little Surrey train, note it's leaving right lines (7)*

'Runaway' suggests there's an anagram here. 'Little Surrey

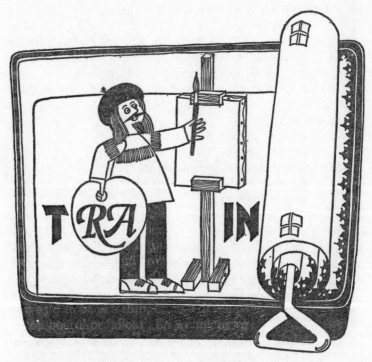

Put the famous artist in the can for discipline

train' gives us 'Sy–train', of which an anagram is 'str–a–y–i–n'. Now we *ignore the comma* and add the 'g', or 'note', to complete the word. So we are left with the definition, 'it is leaving the right lines'.

The foregoing examples emphasize once again the need to be prepared to take every word and every part of a word in the clue quite literally. And, if there is an acrobatic clue there, to close our eyes to the punctuation, just as we sometimes have to do with hidden words and anagrams.

> *Country-lover Irishman hugs threesome* (7)
> answer: *patriot* (*pa–trio–t*)
> *Cured the abstainer, being immersed in ale!* (6)
> answer: *better* (*be–TT–er*)

The abstainer, or teetotaller (TT) is immersed in 'beer', or ale. Cured=better.

So far most of the clues have stated, either directly or by a metaphor, that one word is within another. There are times, however, when there may be an implication, rather than a statement.

A frequent illustration of this principle is the use of the word 'bed' (and, less frequently, 'cot'). Countless small words can be enclosed in 'bed', thus: b–ox–ed; b–oil–ed; b–att–ed; b–rave–ed.

Suppose we take 'b–eli–ed'. The compiler might decide that this is Eli, the prophet, in bed. But instead of saying so, he might tell us that 'the prophet' is 'at rest'. In other words we must *picture* him being *in* 'bed'. Another example:

> *Remarks of thousand men at rest* (8)
> answer: *comments* (*co–Mmen–ts*)

i.e., a thousand ('M') men are in their 'cots'. The outcome is 'comments', or remarks.

This principle may be applied also in other directions. It is often used in regard to ships and sailing, especially where the compiler is using 's.s.' as an abbreviation for 'steamship'. A person or object enclosed by 'ss', such as 's–ham–s' or s–nob–s, is said to be *in* a ship, or, as a development from that, to be 'on board' or 'afloat'. So we might be given 'Kim, afloat' for 'skims'; 'pray on board' for 'sprays'.

Test Word 11

(Solution on page 106)

Across

6 Longing to embroil fist with West upper left (7)
7 Put off ye lad in a flummox (5)
9 Name in air comes to novice, Burrow (6)
10 That is, Southern journal in pictures (6)
11 Chewing I cast badly at one in county (11)
13 In exultation sailor has alternative embroidery (11)
17 Din shattering, I go blue (6)
18 Without difficulty each one put in sly surroundings (6)
19 Unmarried, in fun we delight (5)
20 Buffalo Bill taking upper class saint into imprisonment (7)

Down

1 Without Monsieur in United States (5)
2 Sat awkwardly getting last letter in North America verse (6)
3 Order full probe to become slug-resistant (6,5)
4 Leave haphazard trade about pence (6)
5 Note troubled honour in pay for Buttons (4,3)
8 Di's company joins the shortened queue where records spin (11)

12 Soaring quietly, old convict takes in ruined pub (7)
14 Ring the Italian resting with heightened temperature (6)
15 Sent astray in outsize attacks (6)
16 French writer left in a glance (5)

10

Up and Down and Backwards

There are a number of words whose spelling reads the same both backwards and forwards; they are called Palindromes. Ada, Eve, civic, rotor, minim are a few examples.

Sometimes an entire phrase or sentence may be palindromic. "Madam, I'm Adam!" and "Able was I ere I saw Elba" are among the more renowned palindromes. The longest one I have come across, presumably uttered at a banquet by a conscious-stricken diner, is "Desserts I desire not, so long no lost one rise distressed." A noble sentiment, indeed, if something of a mouthful!

Compilers make the most of palindromes. A word like 'level' can be described as being 'the same whichever way you look at it'; a 'nun' is the same as she goes to and fro; 'refer' is the same word 'backwards or forwards'; 'redder' looks the same 'in both directions', and so on.

This is only the start to reading words backwards. In puzzles, the practice may not be limited to palindromes; it may also apply to other words, syllables, or abbreviations. The compiler will tell us when he wants us to read, or write, something backwards, saying that such-and-such 'returns', is 'taken aback', or 'is coming back', or 'retreats', or is 'in reverse', etc. (In a more advanced puzzle he may even say that something goes 'from east to west', on the premise that

normal English text runs from left to right, or west to east.)
  Some simple examples to start with:

> *Backward step for favourites* (4)
> *answer: pets*

or 'favourites', written backwards.

> *Women's Institutes send back for a place in Lancs* (6)
> *answer: Widnes* (*W.I.*–dnes)

an abbreviation, plus 'send' written *back*.

  Now for a few less obvious examples:

> *Friendlier relations take back rebel* (6)
> *answer: kinder* (*kin–deR*)

'Friendlier' is a description of 'kinder'. Relations, or 'kin', *take back* the 'red', or traditional rebel.

> *Bus returns, so does Emil, all exalted!* (7)
> *answer: sublime* (*sub+limE*)

i.e., 'bus' spelt backwards, plus 'Emil' spelt backwards, *all* add up to 'exalted' or 'sublime'.

> *Backward Tom has alternative engine* (5)
> *answer: motor* (*moT–or*)

i.e., 'Tom' spelt backwards has 'or'.

> *Speeding with mixed gin after reversing car* (6)
> *answer: racing* (*rac–ing*)

'Speeding'='racing'. It is made *with* an anagram of 'gin' *after* spelling 'car' backwards.

  In all the foregoing examples we have been more or less *told* to look for backward spelling. In more difficult cryptic puzzles we may find that the hint itself is wrapped up. Instead of 'backward Thomas' we may see 'turnabout Thomas'. As it's always considered fair to abbreviate names like this, it may become backward Tom or m–o–t. In such a way, 'turn-about Tom touches toes' would give 'mottoes'.

  Still more oblique hints of the backward ploy may take the form of clues telling us something is 'mirrored' or 're-flected'. If we read that 'Elba is reflected' in something we will know that the word or syllable we are looking for is 'able'.

  Where a word is of two or more syllables, we may find only half of it is manipulated in reverse (as in our examples for 'Widnes', 'kinder', 'kindred', 'motor' and 'racing'.) It is possible, however, to have the whole word broken into reversed sections (as we saw in the example for 'sublime') or even whole phrases. But, unlike 'sublime', where the reverses were *stated* – i.e., 'bus' and 'Emil' – we may have some synonyms. For example:

> *Gloomy Sid returns, having hit back* (6)
> *answer: dismal* ('*Sid*' back + '*lam*' back)

Here, although 'Sid' was stated, we had to find a synonym of 'hit', namely 'lam'. Or again:

> *Little modern turn-coats get back top stage status* (7)
> *answer: stardom* ('*mod. rats*' backwards)

Here we had to abbreviate 'little modern' to 'mod' and also change 'turn-coats' to 'rats', then the whole lot *gets back* to spell 'stardom', or top status on the stage.

In the last chapter we studied the acrobatics of syllables and abbreviations. Now we can carry the acrobatic principle a stage farther, putting *backward* words and abbreviations inside forward ones – and vice versa. Thus:

> *Detectives return during repast for a health check* (7)
> *answer: medical* (*me–DIC–al*)

In crosswords, 'detectives' generally, or 'police department' in particular, are often abbreviated to CID (Criminal Investigation Department.) Here CID is put backwards into 'meal', or 'repast'. 'A health check' defines 'a medical'.

> *Put back snare, indeed, and went off* (8)
> *answer: departed* (*de–part–ed*)

A more difficult one, this. We begin by ignoring the commas. Then we *put back* 'trap' (a synonym of 'snare') so that it becomes 'part'. Now the reversed snare goes *in* 'deed' (a compiler's trick) to make 'departed', or 'went off'.

> *Gracious! Jonson's swallowed drink the wrong way* (6)
> *answer: benign* (*Be–nig–n*)

This clue uses a number of ploys to be found in cryptic puzzles. It starts by putting us off the scent, with that exclamation mark. If we ignore it, we can turn 'gracious' into a definition of 'benign'. We have seen earlier how famous people can be alluded to by their Christian names. As he has 'swallowed' something we should know that this Jonson's first name must be only three or four letters long – not too hard to find 'Ben'. We can soon make him *swallow* 'gin' (a drink) the wrong way round.

Now for down clues. Their solutions, being written and read from top to bottom, can perform acrobatic tricks denied to the horizontal ones.

When answers, or parts of answers, are read backwards vertically – that is, upwards – they are often said to be 'climbing', 'going up to', 'upwards', 'rising', or simply 'up'. Or one part of the word may be said to be 'over' or 'above' another, or 'under' or 'beneath' it. Sometimes the bottom part of the word may be said to be 'supporting' or 'propping up' the first part. It is all part of the process of taking *literally* the physical arrangement of letters and syllables.

Below are some examples of what might be solutions to 'down' clues. If we relate them to the sample clues which follow we will get a better idea of how this ploy works.

1	*2*	*3*	*4*
S	D	T	S
U	E	A	T
B	N	B	E
			W

1 *Small payment for overturned bus* (3)
   answer: sub

'Bus' is upsidedown, giving 'sub', a small, or abbreviated, form of subscription or subsidy, i.e., payment.

2 *Study Ned doing a somersault* (3)
   answer: den

'Den', in crosswords, is often equated with a study (a private office or glory hole). Here 'Ned' is visually head-over-heels.

3 *Label for upside-down upside-down sleeper?* (3)
   answer: tab

'Tab' can be a kind of 'label'. The bat (its reversed spelling) sleeps upside-down, of course.

4 *Soaks up what may simmer down* (4)
   answer: stew

Up, the answer reads 'wets'. Read down, it is 'stew', something that simmers.

As in 'across' clues and solutions, we may also meet

acrobatics in the 'down' ones, involving reverse spellings placed inside forward ones, or adjoining them. Fortunately our sportsman of a compiler will always give us an indication of which part of the word is to be read backwards or upwards. Again, here are some possible solutions to 'down' clues:

1	2	3	4	5	6
P	C	P	D	E	S
E	A	L	I	Y	P
R	R	E	A	E	I
S	R	A	G	S	N
O	O	S	R	O	E
N	T	E	A	R	T
			M	E	T
					E

1 *Somebody's boy is supporting rising rep* (6)
   answer: *person*

'Person' = 'somebody'. 'Rising rep' is 'per' spelt down in the orthodox way; 'son' is a boy supporting, or holding up 'rep'.

2 *Car hillclimbing gets donkey's reward* (6)
   answer: *carrot*

'Carrot' is the 'donkey's reward'. We *get* it by 'car', presented normally, and 'tor', or hill, *climbing* to spell r–o–t.

3 *Turn the record over the rest to give pleasure* (6)
   answer: *please*

'Please' = 'to give pleasure'. 'LP' (long playing) is a brief way of saying record or Disc. Turn it – i.e., PL – *over* 'ease' or 'rest'.

4 *Plan to take up aid with King George before noon* (7)
   answer: *diagram*

'Plan' defines the 'diagram'. 'Dia' is 'aid' taken *up*. It is *with* 'GR' (King George) and 'am' (before noon).

5 *Viewer meets Cupid climbing, not a pretty sight!* (8)
   answer: *eyesore*

'Viewer' is an 'eye', something that looks or views. It meets 'Eros' (Cupid) climbing, or spelt *upwards*, making 'eyesore' – not a pretty sight!

6 *Old instrument makes ten rise up in malice* (8)
   answer: *spinette*

A 'spinette' is an old musical instrument. 'Ten' spelt upwards in 'spite' (or malice) makes the answer.

Rising skill in making part of bridal gown

Test Word 12 (Solution on page 107)

Across

6 Knock-out reversal contributes to paralytic attack (6)
7 Nip back finally with this composer (6)
8 Research into tangled vines; no, I tag it back (13)
9 Wilt a crowd with poor return (5)
10 Indian coin each way for her (4)
11 Walker's way to tap back hard (4)
14 Returns to slumber and strips (5)
16 With renewed alibi it probes the likelihoods (13)
18 Advertised a liberal come-back and went ahead (6)
19 On reflection dole is crazy for one in the soup (6)

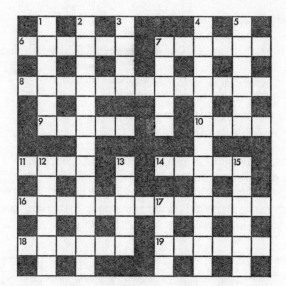

Down

1 A not upcoming editor made restitution (6)
2 Caddie's invitation to the dance? (4,2,3,4)
3 Pour up to Hunt's starting-point (4)
4 Infringement of art held up in a fashion (13)
5 Cut off, Sid somersaulted, now upset (6)
7 Havanna makes Channel Islands get rag up (5)
12 Scared of making a loud incursion (6)
13 Went by Underground for the upward launching (6)
15 Coldly hard Scottish list of candidates turning up in Surrey (6)
17 The Orient props up nothing rank (4)

Test Word 13 (Recap)   (Solution on page 108)

Across

1 Ahem! Rather short for the seventies? (4-5)
5 Secret clique gets graduate into a State (5)
8 Droop when gas comes back (3)
9 Something laid up for what the future may hatch (4-3)

11 Very little money, so what's done? (3)
12 You'll find him in 'Stoic Lives' (5)
14 Where the English found a French Maid bewitching (7)
16 Scottish town arranged to kill crew without Lot (7)
18 A mixture of entertainment (7)
20 Fire-dog is also a club (7)
22 Metal mass got in transposition (5)
24 Fool of a ship (3)
25 Daniel enters before the slow movement (7)
27 Boring instrument of muddled legislation (3)
28 Hundred came in order to build holy city (5)
30 Having been charged with gas and air (7)
32 Desperate alternatives from outdoor dietarian (2,2,3)
33 Keenly, for example, turning in early (7)

Down
 1 Harmoniously sum up, in charge with partner (9)
 2 Scold the horse (3)
 3 Scorch, having mixed spirit in the South-East (5)

4   Available in thin stockings (2,5)
5   Wheel tooth shows nothing in centre of gravity (3)
6   Fish swallows one fundamental ingredient (5)
7   Washing makes lady run all over the place (7)
10 Animate in seven live numbers (7)
13 But such incursions could be made across fields (7)
15 Traffic system with high-flown objectives (3,4)
17 Article in India? It's in the U.S. .... (7)
19 ... and follows ruined glen as part of U.K. (7)
21 Colourful binding, but may tie things up for too long
      (3,4)
23 Longfellow's chest? (7)
24 Directed me in assistance (5)
26 Foster sister possibly (5)
29 Dovelike sound we hear with Bill (3)
31 Pull violin string up (3)

I I

Sounds, English and Foreign

It is possible to pair up numerous words which have completely different spellings and meanings and which have the same, or nearly the same, pronunciation or sound: read–reed, Jean–gene, side–sighed, blue–blew, maid–made, least–leased, for just a few examples.

Sometimes a compiler will *use* one spelling while *alluding* to another. When he does so his secondary clue may tell us that 'we hear' or 'it sounds like' something, or a word or phrase 'echoes' another of little or no related meaning. Taking 'side' and 'sighed' the clue might be:

> *Team was a little weary, we hear (4)*
> answer: *side* (sighed)

To make it less easy the compiler might have substituted Eleven were . . .' or 'XI were . . .', or even:

> *Sounds as if this team lost hope* (4)
> *answer: side (sighed)*

'This team' is the definitive clue, whereas the whole sentence offers the secondary clue.

The lesson is that any reference to what our clue may sound like when *read aloud* should make us look for an answer which, if spoken, could mean something else. Some more examples of sound effects:

> *Old diarist is a snooper, by the sound of him* (5)
> *answer: Pepys (peeps)*

In other words, it sounds as if old Samuel Pepys is a 'peeper'.

With experience it becomes easy to work out straight-forward sound-effect clues, but when it comes to phrases it can be a trickier matter. This is where the compiler enjoys himself, sometimes using a little licence as to pronunciation, (so we mustn't be too pedantic when we analyse some of the results). Here are some examples:

> *Venerate lazy viewers, we hear* (7)
> *answer: idolize ('idle eyes', we hear)*
> *'Out of stock' echoes a singular misgiving* (4,5)
> *answer: sold out ('sole doubt' echoed)*

Now for a more involved example, which might be found in harder cryptic puzzles:

> *Sounds as if a chord is forbidden to these bowed musicians* (6,4)
> *answer: string band*

It sounds as if a string or cord (which echoes 'chord') is banned (which echoes 'band'). 'These' indicates that the 'bowed musicians' are the definitive clue. And 'bowed' may have put us off the scent (the word could easily have been 'bowing'). Here it means 'musicians with bows', for playing their violins, *not* that they are bent double.

While we are on the subject of sound effects we might jump ahead a little to a type of clue elaborated in chapter twelve. For instance, we might be startled to see a clue like this:

> *E E (to relax soundly)* (2,4)
> *answer: to ease*

We see two 'E's. We *say* 'Two E's' . . . and we *hear* 'To ease', or to relax.

Similarly 'T T' might be used to indicate 'to tease'. Such trick clues aren't so difficult to solve, especially when we have some 'holding' letters already filled in.

Sometimes compilers introduce what might be called 'distorted' sounds in the form of local dialects or alternative national (often Scottish) pronunciations of English words. An example of the latter is 'ain', possibly described as 'Scot's own'.

VERY In French = $\begin{array}{l} \text{TRAI} \\ \text{TRÈS} \end{array}\bigg]$ N North Pole

Peacock's tail feathers sound very French to the Pole!

Dropped aitches may be used, usually with a reference to Cockney pronunciation. For instance, 'all, as the Cockney might say', could be 'hall'. Example:

> *Soothing way Cockney says he's over-eaten?* (7)
> *answer: easeful ('e's full' in Cockney speech)*

Sometimes a clue may tell us that somebody is speaking 'commonly' or 'vulgarly'. It could indicate a dropped aitch, but is more likely to mean that the answer involves some slang meaning. 'Common gaol' might mean 'clink', 'nick', 'quod' or 'stir'. 'Vulgar' money could be interpreted as 'quid', 'dough', 'fiver', etc. 'Food commonly' could be 'nosh', 'grub' or even 'bangers', and so on.

'Colloquially speaking' may also be inserted into a clue thus making slang and figures of speech sound more acceptable than 'vulgarly' and 'commonly'. It may refer to having a 'snifter', a 'noggin' or 'the other half' for a drink, to watching the 'telly', or taking a spin in the 'jalopy'.

In chapter seven, dealing with abbreviations and contractions, we saw briefly how a few foreign sounds – usually French, Italian, Spanish or German – may creep into our clues occasionally. Here are a few more complex examples:

> *Hoodwinking some French with tiny sound* (6)
> answer: *duping*

i.e., 'du' ('some' in French) with 'ping'.

> *Tell how the Spanish is caught by speed* (6)
> answer: *relate* (*r–el–ate*)

'The' in the Spanish language is 'el'. It is caught in 'rate', or 'speed', to give 'relate', or 'tell'.

Numbers may be imported, too. 'One German' might become 'eine, ein'; 'two Spanish' may be 'dos'; 'three Italian 'tre', etc. Thus:

> *Checks King with one German point* (5)
> answer: *reins* (*R–ein–S*)

'Checks' = 'reins'. Made from 'R' (abbreviation for rex) + 'ein' or 'one' in German, and 's' or compass point.

> *Inferred the French nobleman got into the act* (7)
> answer: *deduced* (*de–Duc–ed*)

'Duc', or French nobleman, has got into 'deed', or the act.

There are times when a clue may only *imply* a foreign word by referring to a town or country where it might be used. 'Two in Spain' could again be 'dos'. 'Parisian boy' could be 'garçon', a 'street in Marseilles' just 'rue'. 'Ancient Roman law' would probably be 'lex'.

> *Intricate competition with law in ancient Rome* (7)
> answer: *complex* (*comp–lex*)

'Intricate' = 'complex'. ('Competition' abbreviated.)

Test Word 14 (Solution on page 109)

Across

1 The animal sounds as if it has many holes to sink (4)
5 Utterly appropriate the oceans (4)
7 Clothing that Ray intended, we hear (7)
8 Victim may do so on knees, 'tis said (4)
10 Drive-off point sounds refreshing (3)
11 Window glass can hurt pronouncedly (4)
13 Senior takes heart to heart, being winner of points (6)
15 A score for five quartets? (6)
17 Theologian in a slipper is a mess (6)
19 Kind of trance of a Greek island (6)
20 He makes to go back and forth . . . (4)
22 . . . and she's the same to and fro (3)
23 Say it if the glass is high enough (4)
25 Audibly sited, and can see, too (7)
26 The selling of sound canvas sheet (4)
27 Flier echoes merit (4)

Down

1 Be utterly imperfect over nineteenth letter (4)
2 Such a photograph shows what can't be seen (1-3)

3 Strain a potion, as they say (6)
4 Modest descent, having lost old Bob (6)
5 Tread the Russian plain, we hear (4)
6 The place heard in 25 across (4)
9 But *does* this stringed implement make such a din? (7)
12 Chemical's special pay for late shift, by the sound of it (7)
14 Colour soundly perused (3)
16 You echo the sheep (3)
18 Reappear from *mal de mer* genteelly (6)
19 Century warms the frauds (6)
20 Hours, 'tis said, belong to us (4)
21 River's pronounced slimy mud (4)
23 Walk through water utterly balanced (4)
24 Sniffer sounds knowledgeable (4)

I 2

Adding and Subtracting

In his endless search to find new ways of writing clues for familiar words the compiler sometimes resorts to the trick of extending a word so that, to find the solution, we have to cut it down to size again. When he has done so, the compiler usually tells us the word 'loses' part of itself, or is 'decapitated' (if it loses a first letter), or is 'shortened', or possibly 'drops' a letter or syllable, to give the required result. Or again, the word may be 'disheartened', if the middle has to go, or 'endless' if its tail must be disposed of. Various other hints may be given.

Suppose a clue is being written for 'eel', that perennially slippery customer haunting the crossword squares. Like most three-letter words (and there aren't a great many of them) this one offers limited scope; there's not much any compiler can do with 'eel' that hasn't been done scores of times already. So he may first extend the word to 'peels', thus:

> *Slippery customer peels away the postscript* (3)
> *answer: eel*

i.e., we have been given 'peels' and told to take *away* the 'PS' (postscript) to find our slippery customer.

Below are a few illustrations of phrases indicating that words must be cut down to size to produce something entirely different.

Phrase	Part removed	Remaining solution
restore no mineral	'ore' (*mineral*) from restore	*rest*
Earnest loses a listener	'ear' (*listener*) from Earnest	*nest*
disheartened peddler	'ddl' (*the heart of peddler*)	*peer*
parson lost his head	'p' (*the head, or beginning, of parson*)	*arson*
pointless rage	'e' (*rage less a compass point*)	*rag*
Freda, dropping article	'a' (*article dropped from Freda*)	*Fred*
forgive no teatime	'iv' ('*teatime*' not in forgive)	*forge*

Although we may see quite easily how the solutions in the last column are arrived at, we must ask ourselves: would we recognize the phrase in the first column for what it was, *if it were incorporated in a full length clue?* For this is the trick we must learn to master. Here are some complete examples.

> *After director has left, dirtier row seen* (4)
> *answer: tier*

Here 'dir' (an abbreviation of 'director') *has left* 'dirtier', when 'tier' (or 'row)' is seen to remain. (The punctuation here can be misleading. The trick is to make an imaginary shifting of the comma so that the construction of the clue would be: 'after director has left dirtier, row seen.') Incidentally, 'row' is one of these words which often cause solvers to jump to the wrong conclusions! It has many meanings apart from a 'noise' or 'quarrel'.

Practise straining not to make a song

> *Make a song about a shilling with no rise* (4)
>   *answer: sing*

Here 's–hill–ing' loses its 'hill', or 'rise'.

Looking ahead to more difficult cryptic puzzles for advanced solvers we may find that an abstraction of part of a word is implied rather than stated. Our 'shilling' in the last example might have become a *'flattened* shilling', that is a string of letters without a 'hill' in them. A 'levelled hill fort' might refer to a simple 'fort' whose 'hill' has been levelled away. Again, the abstraction might be given the gimmicky treatment (discussed more fully in a later chapter), thus:

> *Carry the beggar who lost a sound horse* (4)
> answer: *bear*

'Bear', or carry, is made from 'be–gg–ar' who has *lost* 'gg' (which has the *sound* of 'gee-gee', or horse).

Reverting to our more usual cryptic clues, we will also find that the pieces of a word to be cut out need not necessarily be together. The compiler might hint that they are not. 'Haggle, no egg components . . .' would leave us with 'Hal' (possibly the Bluff King) after 'g–g–e', the *components* of 'egg', had gone.

But we can't rely on being told that the 'surplus' letters are split. For example:

> *Printed without colour but in demand at the bar* (4)
> answer: *pint*

'A pint' is in demand in the pub. Achieved by 'printed' without 'r–ed' or colour; note the missing letters were split up in the original word.

Now we turn to a different use of the 'adding and subtracting' ploy. This is when the compiler doesn't tell us what his extension is, but resorts to hypothesis. If such-and-such a thing were added, he says, the result would be so-and-so. Supposing he were writing a clue for 'leader' (of men). He might tell us he was adding 'ring' to the solution, and then give us a clue for that. Thus:

> *If he follows a ring his band must be up to mischief!* (6)
> answer: *leader*

When working out the answer we come to 'ringleader' fairly easily. The 'If' having told us that he doesn't really follow 'ring', it is but a short step to cut it down to our 6-letter solution, 'leader'.

> *If he had another ten, his legs would still be three* (3)
> answer: *Manx*

In this clue 'he' tells us we are looking for a male. What male has three legs? Man, the Isle of, immediately comes to mind. Give him an 'x' (ten more) and he is 'Manx'.

> *If he started with an egg would he make a cleverer boss?* (4)
> answer: *head*

Here we know that 'he' must be some kind of boss already because we are asked to consider whether he could be a cleverer one. What sort of clever people start with an 'egg'? Egg-heads, of course. But he *doesn't* start with one, which leaves us with 'head'.

Test Word 15

(Solution on page 110)

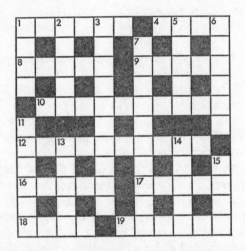

Across

1　Bound with handsprings after workers departed (6)
4　Tramped having lost Ted where slope is (4)
8　Madman drops penny of old French mum (5)
9　Lusty air from dozen operas restaged without drapes (5)
10　Pound me in instant part of serial (10)
12　If meeting had no work unit nunnery would survive (10)
16　Public overture cut flower (5)
17　Quartz the Aga tensely grips (5)
18　Falsely replies there's no material (4)
19　Let as pleased, not soft-headed (6)

Down

1　Sumptuous pit chucked us out! (4)
2　Italian romance cut out civil engineer (5)

3 The golfer's easiest hole last century (10)
5 Solitary Malone has lost a thousand (5)
6 Attractive prey taking in abstainer (6)
7 Organization of Galileo, etc., like a college (10)
11 Such masters are mostly cool (6)
13 Relative sort of nice tea? No, thanks! (5)
14 Oddly answers no South-West approaches (5)
15 Pendragon, nude, to hang in the balance (4)

Test Word 16 (Recap)   (Solution on page 111)

Across

1 Old Bob, sick at sea . . . (7)
4 . . . might obtain water supply to be cured (3,4)
7 Learner up in a bloomer (5)
9 An escape that sometimes makes news (7)
11 Make hay, boy! (3)

13   Pop in ad. designed for college outsider (7)

15   Snake feathers in coil (3)

17   Briefly cut horticulture in cunning enclosure (7)

19   The bold shows singular one; the scared shows its plural (5)

20   Hurried round beam but got sprinkled (7)

22   Disappointment when dress is outgrown? (3-4)

24   Fawner twisted inside at this date (5)

26   Old l ac. craft cripple rebuilt (7)

28   Jack left the tarmac to get rainwear (3)

30   Cowered from horrific ring, edging away (7)

32   Rue the turbulent current (3)

33   It's apples, rehashed as dried veg (5,4)

34   Women's Institute study to expand (5)

Down

1   Divide the rent (5)

2   One member's wicked spirit (3)

3   Got a lip twisted with kind of turpentine (7)

4   But the humblest parents could become so magnificent (5)

5   Ate disturbing meal (3)

6   Bags the trunks (7)

8   Go on, Ely! Make new word-meanings (7)

10   In Latin, therefore, BMA concocted ban (7)

12   Wanted team mixed over the German rising (7)

14   Uninterrupted French refusal to arrest (3-4)

16   High speeds for periods of abstinence (4,5)

18   Howling Yukon leader takes the Spanish fish (7)

21   To mislead a crowd engulfed in river I've following (7)

23   Sort of stuff to make the girl wail (7)

25   l ac. craft perhaps (5)

27   Tyro, under training, holds ring (5)

29   Pass between peaks (3)

31   We'd rise for early freshness (3)

13

Linked Clues and Quotations

We have devoted a lot of effort so far to breaking up words and phrases and reassembling them like jigsaw puzzles. Now we will concentrate more on the various meanings of words in their entirety, and on clues which deal more broadly with the relationship of words to each other.

Again we start with the easiest examples, namely the straight quotations and 'linked' clues, left aside until now because they will lead us more naturally into the field of association of ideas to be explored at the next stage.

For solvers with good memories, or with a handy book of quotations at their elbow, the completing of 'quotation' clues can prove useful for starting off a puzzle and a godsend in getting a move on with a really difficult one. Of course it's often possible to solve many such clues by guesswork, once a few linking answers have been written into the square.

Many solvers find 'linked' clues more interesting. The simplest form is where two consecutive clues are linked by groups of dots, indicating that they have a common association of ideas in their development – although the solutions may be quite unrelated to each other. (In fact, this book cheated a little in starting off the last Test Word, No. 16, with a couple of 'linked clues'.) Here is an example of an idea which is not so immediately obvious:

> 8. ac. *Close observer of distant worlds* . . . (*10*)
>   *answer: astronomer*
>
> 9. ac. . . . *sharing experience with floored pugilist?* (*6,5*)
>   *answer: seeing stars*

These two clues, of course, would be consecutive in the puzzle. Although their subjects have no connection, the way the solutions are worded provides an association of ideas.

However, it is not unusual for widely separated clues to have cross-references to each other. Suppose we read this:

> *14. ac.*   *He works with planes in woods* (9)
>   answer: *carpenter*

(i.e., 'planes', or carpenter's tools, in 'woods' or materials) – we may not get the answer immediately. In the same puzzle the clue for, say, 19 down, might read:

> *With 14 ac. he wept by the sea* (6)

Not until we have solved 14 across can we 'translate' 19 down into:

> *With (the) carpenter he wept by the Carroll sea* (6)

whereupon we will know with certainty that the answer is 'walrus'. (For who does not know of Lewis Carroll's strange pair who walked along the briny beach and 'wept like anything to see such quantities of sand'?)

'. . . *a tree when it is young*' – proverb

So far so good. But there may be occasions when several clues are linked by their numbers only. Suppose, instead of the above clues for walrus and carpenter, we saw the following in the same puzzle:

> *14 ac.*   See 7 *down* (9)
> *19 dn.*   See 7 *down* (6)
> *7 dn.*   *Molluscs eaten by 19 dn. and 14 ac. amid floods of tears* (7)
>   *answer: oysters*

It really wouldn't take us long to guess that the molluscs in question were 'oysters'; from there it is a short stage to work out what *couple* ate oysters amid tears.

Incidentally, cross-referenced clues may be made more difficult by not including the words 'down' and 'across', or their abbreviations. It is the style of some puzzles, such as *The Daily Telegraph*'s, to mention these only where there are both Down and Across clues with the same number.

For example, if there were only a 10 Across clue to a puzzle, and no 10 Down, a clue for 'carpenter' might read: 'With 10 he wept . . .' etc. So the solver would have to work out whether '10' referred to another clue or to a meaning of the numeral or indeed whether it might imply 'x' or 't–e–n' spelt out.

Test Word 17   (Solution on page 112)

Across

1 Where standard is in a fix up North (2,3,4)
5 Case for the 11 when travelling by 24 down? (5)
8 Little Neddy returns to lair (3)
9 Uppish thug tumbling in hay (7)
11 Imitate the primate (3)
12 '. . . a proud —— on so proud a back' – Shakespeare, *Venus and Adonis* (5)
14 'Total ——, without all hope of day!' – Milton, *Samson Agonistes* (7)
16 Among the pampas Saul tried to attack (7)
18 Magnetic sketch? (7)
20 Though placid it yields hidden sourness (7)
22 Urge one member to join the Spanish (5)
24 Stuff for 18 on? (3)
25 Thrown off, the object of 13, perhaps . . . (7)

27 . . . because of such age? (3)
28 Bedeck the Fleet after much fuss (5)
30 'Will all great —— 's ocean wash this blood clean from my hand?' – Shakespeare, *Macbeth*, Act II (7)
32 Hug the doctor backing car between points (7)
33 No more French puzzle (7)

Down

1 Pledge to conduct a funeral (9)
2 Brown on 10, maybe (3)
3 'An ampler ——, a diviner air' – Wordsworth, *Laodamia* (5)
4 Rich little work, classy, with fast time (7)
5 Small company, rather shy (3)
6 A labyrinth to astonish (5)
7 'O thou art fairer than the —— air' – Marlow, *Faustus* (7)
10 A break taken in 30's company, possibly (7)
13 Sid comes up with domino to throw away (7)

15   'Don't shoot the —, he's doing his best' – Anon. (7)
17   I con NUR into a one-horned arrangement (7)
19   Entreat little demon to take learning (7)
21   Emotional outcome of mixing in teens (7)
23   Boarding-house dwellers who could be taking 10 (7)
24   A trident, perhaps – but nothing like 30's (5)
26   '. . . variable as the shade By the light quivering —
      made' – Sir Walter Scott, *Marmion* (5)
29   Back little brother, giving the eye (3)
31   Vase to merit, we hear (3)

14

Allusions and Delusions

In our everyday conversation we are constantly using figures
of speech which add life and colour to what we are saying.
There are thousands of phrases whose literal and metaphorical meanings are completely different. To take just
four commonplace examples:

'*fell off*'   Literally, *the can fell off the shelf.*
          Metaphorically, *the factory output of
          cans fell off.*

'*dropped in*'   Literally, *the penny was dropped in the
          hat.*
          Metaphorically, *his colleague was
          dropped in the mire*
          or, *our friends dropped in unexpectedly.*

'*pulled his leg*' Literally, *stretched the limb (possibly
          to put it in a splint).*
          Metaphorically, *told him a tall story.*

'*ring off*'   Literally, *end a telephone call*
          or, *(broken engagement) ring off the
          finger.*

The last example, of course, is one of two different literal interpretations of the phrase. If we sat down to write a list of colourful expressions or idioms in regular use we would be at the job for days. Our list might start with: pick holes in, turn the tables, trim one's sails, hit the nail on the head, come a cropper, get the wind up, catch a packet, led up the garden, put a spoke in his wheel, up against a brick wall, give him an inch . . ., full of beans, come up trumps, take the biscuit, old hat, when his ship comes home, holding the baby . . . and so on, and so on.

A Rocket of thought in George Stephenson's case?

The point is that all these phrases present an opportunity for the compiler to write one clue that may relate to both meanings, or possibly to take one meaning and make a pun of it. We saw some simple illustrations of the former in chapter three on 'multiple definitions'. Now we take the whole principle several stages further.

Suppose the clue is for 'high hat', which could, in crossword terms, be a 'tall hat' but which, in dictionary terms, was originally the wearer of a top-hat and now means a snob or aristocrat or one who puts on airs. The compiler could amuse himself by using the lot, writing:

Snobby titfer? (*4-3*)
answer: high-hat

Having used the Cockney rhyming-slang 'titfer' for 'hat' he can take the Cockney's eye view of a high-hat as a snob (person) or snobby wear.

When both a literal and a figurative interpretation are used in the same clue we will frequently find that it ends with a question mark. The compiler is hinting that there may be a pun here, or an association of ideas, but that by linking the two together he is either drawing a long bow (if we may permit another metaphor!) or saying that the two *can* be plausibly linked but do not necessarily *have* to be.

Let us have another look at some of the simple examples in chapter three and bring them a stage further:

Forget old quarrels and put on a new face (*4,2*)
answer: make up

By a linking of disconnected ideas we can see two definitions brought to a common solution like this:

Put on a brave face and bury the hatchet? (*4,2*)
answer: make up

A 'brave face' might suggest a Red Indian; to 'bury the hatchet' may also link with Red Indian customs, but is also another metaphor for 'to patch up quarrels'. And *both* in their own ways, mean 'make up'.

Or take the phrase, 'second fiddle'. Literally, it means the second violin, or the man playing it. Figuratively it can mean taking second place, 'playing second fiddle'. One clue might allude to both these meanings. Yet by defining each word separately the compiler could also give the clue an unexpected twist. If he takes 'fiddle' as a slang word for 'fraud' a '*second* fiddle' could be made to mean 'a second swindle'. Following this line of thought this might emerge:

Not the leading violinist's first offence either (*6,6*)
answer: second fiddle

'Either' exercises an important role in this clue. (It's not the first violinist's [and] it's not the first offence.)

Sometimes the clue invites us to imagine a picture which borders on the absurd, for example:

> *Fed up – but didn't he pluck the chicken first?* (4,2,3,5)
> *answer: down in the mouth*

Well, the first definitive, part of that clue was enough to give us the answer anyway!

> *Intellectual with surprised expression?* (8)
> *answer: highbrow*

. . . or he has a raised eyebrow.

We have already learnt how important it is to be ready to see words simply as letters on a page. It is permissible for the compiler to regard the component parts of a word as meaning something quite different from the whole – and to construct a secondary clue based on the alternative meaning.

First, a few examples of such words:

headstone	could be read as	*head's tone*
rusticate		*as rustic ate*
eyesore		*as eyes ore*
stands at ease		*as stands a tease*
discover		*as disc over*

For a simple example of such a clue:

> *Just open a pot* (4)
> *answer: ajar*

– for 'just open' or 'slightly open' is a definition of 'ajar'. And a pot is 'a jar'. Note that the two readings, with the spacing moved, are acceptable. A final '?' may be used where one interpretation of the solution is based on a pun.

> *Manufacturing room for the staff dance?* (8)
> *answer: workshop (works 'hop')*

'Making room' would be an acceptable alternative in some puzzles. A room where manufacture or 'making' is carried on *is* a workshop. Whether or not it might be used for a works hop is a punster's speculation – hence the '?'.

> *Handy treatment for the chap I heal?* (8)
> *answer: manicure (man I cure)*

'Handy treatment', or treatment for the hands, defines the 'manicure'.

And a more obtuse example:

> *Songster who might go off tune after spending one?* (*11*)
> *answer: nightingale (night in gale)*

'Songster' should tell us to look for a bird. The rest follows.

In chapter eleven we saw how a clue can advise us that a word *sounds* like something else with no connected meaning. Now we can carry the same principle to those words and phrases which either have two meanings, or which *would have* two meanings if spelt differently. Such words as:

eyewash	*also sounds like*	*I wash*
tendril		*like ten drill*
spider		*like spied a*
idolize		*like idle eyes*
summertide		*like some are tied*
peregrines		*like Perry grins*

It is hoped that elocutionists will allow us a little latitude in making some of the comparisons.

The 'sound' puns are apt to get themselves incorporated into clues. And we may occasionally meet a clue which will also contain a punning second meaning.

> *I soundly complain it's freezing* (*3,4*)
> *answer: ice cold (I scold – and 'I'se cold!')*

Now 'it's freezing' is a fair definition of ice cold. Also it *soundly* echoes 'I scold' or 'I complain at'. (And here we have the third complaining echo, 'I'se cold!' thrown in as a bonus to make the grammarians' hair curl.)

> *Sounds as if the washerwoman's in despair?* (*8,3,5*)
> *answer: wringing her hands*

At first reading 'sounds' looks like a noun, meaning noises, but here it is a verb; it *implies* that the good lady has been literally wringing the clothes before figuratively 'wringing' her hands.

A variation of this pun:

> *How the despairing campanologist passes the time?* (*8,3,5*)
> *answer: wringing his hands*

Again we have the *implied* fact that the campanologist would normally be 'ringing' the bells.

Test Word 18

(Solution on page 113)

Across

1 Lined paper is, having followed Goethe's 'capital motto' (7,3,5)

7 Giant of a British myth (5)

8 Pertaining to a citizen, anyway (5)

10 Caesar's law inflexions (3)

11 Cretan city where a monster was always amazed? (7)

13 Writer returns for a wine holder (3)

14 One of the onion-seller's overheads? (5)

15 Cover-up brushwork for what's pegged out with pride? (9)

16 Where HE is 'at home' (9)

18 Pied-à-terre, upper-class article, in Italy (5)

20 Corny listener (3)

21 Ford centre of French abstainer taking in foreign royalty (7)

23 Back in Lake – all for nothing! (3)

24 Monastics bullfinches (5)
26 The outcome is 27 (5)
28 Diana's involvement is also undoing (15)
Down
1 Kind of surname a couple of birds might fall for? (6,9)
2 Shadow hound (3)
3 Undetected way to lie without saying a word (5)
4 Her issue is said to be invention (9)
5 A little minister, but some revolutionary! (3)
6 Undisciplined thrills meant end of freedom from bondage* (15)
7 A good one will stir smoothly (5)
9 Snake crushed crab and duck (5)
11 American grasshopper disturbed tidy dak (7)
12 Where the cannibal 'converted' the missionary? (7)
15 Joined the navy out of curiosity, we hear (4,2,3)
17 Scrimmage with science, odd (5)
19 Italian poet died at the stake (5)
22 Crowing with no little credit, being in debt (5)
25 A Gallic turn-down (3)
27 Girl to go to court (3)

*The answer uses the less usual of two alternative spellings.

15

Gimmicks

Although 'gimmicks' has always struck me as being a horrible word I can think of no better one to describe the occasional trick clues which appear in puzzles (and which some compilers will regard as horrible clues). They range from the modestly quirkish, such as:

    *** ||| (5,3,7)
    answer: Stars and Stripes

(which could be the germ of a clue in a respectable puzzle), to something quite outrageous, like:

> *Adriυηω; Aegωvu; Balηω; as sailor sees them ?*(4,4,4)
> answer: half seas over

Gimmick puzzles are as much visual puzzles as they are word puzzles, which is probably why purists and pedants fight shy of them. Even so, they can be fun; borderline examples may be found in all puzzles, and no guide would be complete without some reference to them. Suppose we saw this:

> * * * *They won the jackpot* (5,5)

would we get the answer? The asterisks, we know, are popularly called 'stars'. If they took the jackpot, in 5 and 5 letters, the answer must surely be 'lucky stars' (although, for a fruit machine's jackpot, it might as well be 'three stars').

Or what about this, in similar vein?

> *20. 20. Best way to dart out!* (6,3)

We might begin by recalling that 20.20. in continental time is 'eight twenty' by the British clock – but the letters wouldn't fit. So we might consider that 20.20 is also *double* twenty, which in darts is known as 'double top' (being at the top of the board, and also being the top score possible as a 'double'.) As a darts player must 'go out' with a double score a double top is clearly 'the best way to go out', or, with a pun, to dart out of the game. And so it provides the solution: 'double top'. If we happen not to be darts players, that's just our bad luck!

A respectable gimmick used in quite staid cryptic puzzles is the use of the letter 'o' for 'nothing' in novel ways. It becomes a hollow letter. A 'hungry cat' could end up with a fine 'coat' because the 'c–at' had nothing ('o') in him! An apt place for a 'hungry Scotsman' could be 'moon' because that is 'mon' (Scots *man*) with nothing in him. An inanimate object might be empty rather than hungry. 'Empty bed for a bird' ('cot' with nothing in it) gives us a 'coot'. The letter 'o' gets used in many strange ways. I have even seen 'oo' referred to as 'looking glasses' or 'spectacles'!

Spelling things backwards, without writing a secondary clue, is sometimes resorted to by the most respected compiler. For the gimmick *is* the secondary clue – for example:

Retib (9)

answer: backbiter

i.e., 'biter' *back*(wards).

detcepxenu (*10,7*)

answer: unexpected reverse

i.e., *reverse* the spelling of 'unexpected'.

Finally some gymnastic examples of the kind you won't find in your usual puzzles, but one of their ilk may yet be lurking in a strange cryptic puzzle to snare you!

Niart Alice travelled by?

$\dfrac{ed}{pl}$ *and pillaged* (9)

answer: plundered ('pl' under 'ed')

$\dfrac{L}{S}$ (*beloved round the world*) (6)

answer: lovers (*L*–over–*S*)

For 'all the world loves a Lover', as the saying goes.

$\dfrac{n}{+}$ *Confound!* (7)

answer: nonplus ('n' on '*plus*')

Test Word 19 (Solution on page 114)

(Solution on page 114)

Across

1 seegeeg – how a shirt was lost? (7,6)

6 $\frac{1}{8}$, with staggering effect (3,4,3,5)

13 Some squares exist (3)

15 A matter of sticking together . . . (8)

16 . . . but $\frac{r}{s}$ don't stay put (6)

17 and 25 //// To exercise your body, too (8,4)

20 Ward snag (8)

21 Neared anew to arouse affection (6)

22 Hot pepper taken to Queen with colder result (8)

24 Party ad libber no bread-maker! (3)

26 Powerful effect of introducing live wires? (15)

31 o xxx (we may say in conclusion) (4,3,6)

Down

1 Good French would be sweet if repeated (3)
2 King's Head girl makes Polynesian drink (4)
3 Obtained from the Gothic (3)
4 Raw mineral means nothing to sappers (3)
5 Tonic fifth note (3)
6 $\frac{\text{done}}{\text{and}}$ – and that's that! (4,3,4)
7 Threshed ears for ages (4)
8 Fred lost his head and coloured (3)
9 Just what the ass might be expected to answer! (6)
10 Fiery-chariot rider launched by 23 (6)
11 'But the seamen were not ——; and the —— were not
   seamen.' – Macaulay, *History of England* (9)
12 Three old five-bob pieces for a papal tiara? (6,5)
14 It can be a terrible come-down for those in high places
   (9)
18 Wildly I boost one who plays among reeds (6)
19 One 'cello makes eyelike colour spots (6)
21 The heather is cut for him (4)
23 Hebrew priest upset by falsehood (3)
25 See 17
27 She might be ill (3)
28 Royal Irish Academy exhibiting shortly (1,1,1)
29 A craze in Jaffa dancing (3)
30 Brief operations (3)

Test Word 20 (Recap) (Solution on page 115)

Across

1   Dnoyeb? Not on any map! (3,4,2,6)
9   To court bearing two rings (3)
10   Blimp collapsed, I'd heard (3-4)
11   Returned fee for conveyance (3)
12   An extra clause confused 15 (5)
14   Will has no direction, ailing (3)
15   12 made not so wet (5)
17   Feverish month to aggravate (7)
19   Hand over pie duly rehashed (5,2)
21   Huge maritime disaster (7)
23   They rouse responses (7)
24   Perky extremity Manx cat can't keep (3,2)
26   Law's broken tool (3)
27   A joint on the bishop's head (5)
28   Catch a sheep coming back (3)
30   Be prone to convert wild one (3,4)
31   Implement for 32 at Plymouth (3)
32   Their bloomers may be shown as an example for others (15)

Down

1   Forceful build-up for the battleship's tug? (5,2,8)
2   First person singular (3)
3   Summer twister (5)
4   In the dark he divested the viceroy of Egypt (7)
5   '——, thy name is woman.' Shakespeare, *Hamlet* (7)
6   Objective little Edward finished (5)
7   The world of small brother's return (3)
8   Definitive quality of French text I've given Head (15)
13   Recorded as owing part indeed (7)
16   In and out with two notes involved uncertain outlook (2,5)
18   Scotsman in a triangle (3)
20   Prophet of Peel Island (3)
22   Puss takes water in French castle (7)
23   Full house soundly creates solitary misgiving (4,3)
25   Friend sanctimonious with butterfly feelers (5)

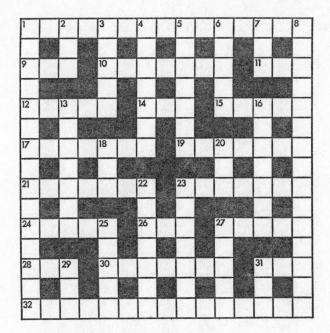

27 Roman disturbed lordly demesne (5)
29 Rodent rising for seaman (3)
31 Royal vessel set out shortly (1,1,1)

Test Word 21 (Recap) (Solution on page 116)

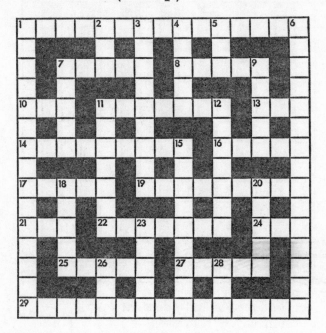

Across

1 Their impressions may influence their readers' opinions (8,7)
7 Bird that can take in Pilot Officer!
8 A throaty bit of suspense (5)
10 For example nothing for oneself (3)
11 Half-baked and non-U ... (3,4)
13 ... and like non-U aunt, a busybody (3)
14 Late meal ready in China ?(6,3)
16 Charge too much for a jab (5)
17 They grow prickly in dry circumstances (5)
19 Anthrax eroder made mask for skin trouble (9)
21 Slack ten follow the French (3)
22 Hope abandoned for what's surrendered (5,2)
24 Has minced tree (3)
25 Where Englishmen feel closest to the French? (5)

27 Persuade me to return quietly in sober state (5)
29 You can't relate to a Shavian title (3,5,3,4)

Down
1 In a perfectly upright fashion (15)
2 Mine's up for gratuity (3)
3 At which a royal telegram is only four years ahead (6-3)
4 He ruled underworld of Greece, but sooner the French, we hear (5)
5 A grounded flier (3)
6 Kind of study of layers in beds (15)
7 He fools around though down at heart (5)
9 On which tellers of old times relied (5)
11 Requiring sound bakery process (7)
12 Slackened off the pressure (5,2)
15 Such an ode is a lament (9)
18 After kiss-in, co-ed steered the course (5)
20 Respond to the theatre's 'Encore'? (5)
23 Artlessly traverse a set of lines (5)
26 I've muddled contest (3)
28 Tripodal island mammal (3)

Solutions, with explanations

In this section the solutions to the Test Words in this book have been set out. Some attempt has been made to supply explanations of the solutions.

TEST WORD No. 1 (page 12)

Across

1 string (cord); held by 'be*st ring*ers'
4 crib (cot); displayed amid 'exoti*c rib*bons'
7 carpet (warm floor covering); 'Red*car pet*shop' has it
8 semi (kind of dwelling); in '*S E Mi*tcham'
10 although (notwithstanding); exposed by 'p*al though*t'
13 cressets (torches); 'massa*cre's set s*cene' includes it
16 Iran (country); 'p*iran*ha' has it
17 sharks (vicious fish); 'Noah's po*sh ark s*helters' them [note 'shelter' does double duty in this clue]
18 gash (nasty cut); in 'stron*g ash*'
19 grated (jarred); contents of 'bi*g rate d*emand'

Down

1 sack (bag); 'crook*s ack*nowledged' hides it
2 rare (underdone); in 'Tund*ra regi*on'
3 needless (unnecessary); 'wasters *need less*on' shows it
5 rueful (sorry); part of '*true ful*filment'
6 bright (shining); in 'Bo*b, right* ahead'
9 thatcher (rural craftsman); seen in 'bes*t hat, Cher*well's'
11 acting (stage performance); in 't*act in G*arden Theatre

12 petals (parts of blossoms); 'lim*pet also*' swallows it
14 trot (jog along); in '*Trot*sky style'
15 used (second-hand); buried in 're*fuse D*on'

TEST WORD No. 2 (page 18)

Across

 6 letter (written message) (permitter)
 7 string (twine) (the stable's racehorses)
 8 Broad (coarse) (Yankee woman) (loved by Norfolk boatmen)
 9 franker (more candid) (marker)
11 thumping (unusually big) (beating)
12 sty (pig pen) (eye sore)
14 egg (urge) (Easter gift)
16 inclined (disposed to) (be slanted)
19 toasted (drank to) (warmly browned)
20 barge (clumsily move) (river freight boat)
22 sneaks (furtively passes) (tale tellers)
23 peeler (policeman) (stripper)

Down

 1 ferret (search out) (a polecat)
 2 stratum (social grade) (layer)
 3 fry (sizzle) (poet Christopher)
 4 crank (faddist) (engine turner)
 5 invest (lay out money) (besiege)
 7 strongly (powerfully) (with concentration)
10 spongers (wipers-up) (parasites)
13 engaged (affianced) (busily occupied)
15 ground (solid land) (crushed to powder)
17 digger (New Zealand miner) (excavator)
18 essay (attempt) (written composition)
21 spy (agent) (spot)

TEST WORD No. 3 (page 27)

Across

 5 late (delayed); tangled t–a–l–e

6   awls (boring instruments); muddled l–a–w–s
8   dub (add sound); new b–u–d
9   eat (consume); new t–e–a
10   death (extinction); crash of h–a–t–e–d
12   spear (pointed weapon); r–e–a–p–s afresh
13   seven (number); oddly e–v–e–n–s
14   feats (exploits); crazy f–e–a–s–t
17   trove (treasure); sorted out voter (elector)
19   smart (fashionable); t–r–a–m–s smashed
20   pot (drug); o–p–t around
22   ill (sick); L–i–l upset
23   soil (earth); from s–i–l–o mixture
24   done (anagram of node)

Down

1   dab (expert); b–a–d arrangement
2   leper (outcast); r–e–p–e–l in confusion
3   warts (skin blemishes); scattered s–t–r–a–w
4   ale (drink); l–e–a disturbed
5   lump (swelling); from squashed p–l–u–m
7   save (rescue); broken v–a–s–e (flower holder)
10   darts (board game); from Strad (valuable violin)
11   heart (a beater); throbbing e–a–r–t–h creates it
15   Eros (Cupid); is s–o–r–e upset
16   smile (joyous look); m–i–l–e–s around
17   trade (commerce); badly r–a–t–e–d
18   vile (horrible); l–i–v–e horribly
21   ton (heavy weight); n–o–t out
22   ink (dark fluid); excited k–i–n

TEST WORD No. 4 (page 29)

Across

1   impeachment (arraignment); 'I'm teen champ' overthrown
6   earl (nobleman); 'Lear' confused
7   angora (Anatolian goat); 'a groan' wildly
9   toneless (without expression); 'lost, seen' wandering
11   straddle (get astride); 'led darts' wildly
13   belays (makes fast); 'sale by' arrangement

14 Avis (girl); 'visa' muddled
15 elementally (by essentials); 'enamel telly' exploded
Down
1 inestimable (incalculable); processing 'sable in time'
2 parent (mother); 'pet ran' amok
3 huntsman (game pursuer); 'maths nun' resolved
4 ebon (hard black wood); chewed 'bone'
5 thanklessly (getting no gratitude); 'hasty knells' wrong
8 flat tyre (deflated tube); 'try a felt' alternatively
10 a devil (a hellish fiend); 'lad I've' tormented
12 flue (up chimney); 'fuel' converted

TEST WORD No. 5 (page 30)

Across
1 glanced (glimpsed) (ricocheted)
4 pacts (agreements); among 'Sho*p Act s*ignatories'
7 tenon (holds with mortise); mixed 'nonet' [anag.]
9 Stour (English river); from 'Alp*s to U*rals'
10 dissemination (scattering [noun]); 'Ted in a mission' [anag.] scattering [verb]
11 dilate (swell out) (speak at length)
12 visage (face); ordered 'G I save'
15 propositional (is being considered); 'on ap*pro, position Al*ec' holds it
18 amend (put right); in the 'be*am end*s'
19 Islam (Mohammedan world); sorted 'mails'
20 emery (polishing powder); used to make 'extr*eme ry*bat'
21 desired (being wanted); 'resided' all over the place
Down
1 gated (curfewed) (with outside entrance)
2 confectionery (sweets); 'try nice cone of' assorted
3 distil (extract essence); from '*Di's til*th'
4 probabilities (likely chances); 'I bit lip as Boer' renewed
5 Corgi (Welsh dog) (motor scooter)
6 silence (hush) (gag)
8 nasal (of the nose); 'Lana's' tweaking
11 deplete (reduce) (exhaust)
13 annul (quash); in 'M*ann, ul*tra-humanist'

14   winded (caught scent) (knocked breathless)
16   orate (harangue); from 'pastor at ease'
17   lamed (crippled); crooked 'medal'

TEST WORD No. 6 (page 36)

Across

1   park (pleasure ground); largely 'ark' (floating menagerie)
8   depressed (in a low state); 'press' is there inside it
9   pride (haughtiness); 'rid' is the heart of the word
10   backlog (work pile-up); 'reverse' (back) with 'ship's record' (log)
11   flock (congregation); mostly 'lock' (shut up)
12   speeder (fast mover); nearly all 'speed' (hurry)
15   ramrods (gun barrel-cleaners); 'ram' (Aries) takes 'rods' (poles)
17   igloo (snow hut); 'I', with 'gloo' (some gloom)
19   amnesty (general pardon); 'am' taking 'nest' (bird home) with 'y' (letter)
20   opted (chose); 'Ted' is major part of the word
22   indecorum (unseemly conduct); taking in 'decor' (stage scenery)
23   yawn (gape); absorbing 'awn' (bit of chaff from barley)

Down

1   petrol (driving spirit); 'pet' with start of 'rolling'
2   producer (film controller); half of it is 'duce' (Italian dictator)
3   asp (snake); 'as' and 'p' (softly) come together as one
4   decamps (makes off secretly); has swallowed 'cam' (Cambridge river water)
6   ambled (sauntered); much of it is 'bled' (blood lost)
7   kangaroo (Australian jumper); has 'gar' (fish) inside
11   formally (with ceremony); 'form' (class) comes to 'ally' (join together)
13   egg spoon (used for breakfast?) anagram of 'Poe's gong'
14   editing (preparing for printer); takes in 'tin'
16   minnow (tiny fish); 'now' (present) ending it

18 open up (undo the doors); 'pen' (writer) is within
21 hew (cut down); 'he' begins the word

TEST WORD No. 7 (page 39)

Across

1 tape (record); starts with variation of 'pat'
3 Sparta (Greek city); hides 'trap' set in another way
7 rota (round of duty); 'oar' broken, and split (by 't')
8 motors (engines); internally, have 'Toro' letters
10 defender (protector); 're-ed' broken at first and last
13 vestment (religious garment); crooked 'stem' inside 've–nt'
16 deride (mock); terribly 'dire' (dreadful) heart of word
17 palm (tropical tree); jagged 'Alp' spells most of it
18 extort (extract); ends with jumbled 'rot'
19 mean (average); mostly made of 'man'

Down

1 tirade (harangue); ends with crazy 'dare'
2 put off (postponed); partly 'pout' about
4 property (estate); ends with confused 'try'
5 riot (disturb peace); 'I' in twisted 'tor'
6 apse (church recess); dominated by angry 'asp'
9 engender (produce); 'green' mixed with broken 'end'
11 debate (discuss); new 'tab' engulfed by river 'Dee'
12 stamen (flower part); finishes with poor 'name'
14 idle (unemployed); start off with wry 'lid' (cover)
15 fret (worry); upset 'ref' makes lot of it

TEST WORD No. 8 (page 47)

Across

7 Panama (American republic); 'pan' (harshly criticize) +'a' 'ma' (little mother)
8 outcry (uproar); 'out' (not in)+'cr' (credit) with 'y' (Yard's leader)
9 completed (all done); 'co' (company)+'MP' (member) and 'le' (the French) join 'Ted'
10 ate (consumed); 'a'+'te' (note, *mus.*)

12 strips (takes off); 'st' (small saint) + 'RIP' + 's' (old Bob)

14 shears (big cutters); 'hear' (harken) between 's–s' (aboard)

15 rather! (yes, indeed!); 'RA' (gunners) taking 'the' 'r' (radius)

17 acorns (oak seeds); 'acor' (anag. of Cora) + 'NS' (opposite poles)

18 odd (strange); 'o' (nothing) to 'DD' (Doctor of Divinity)

19 advertise (announce publicly); 'is averted' muddled (anag.)

22 merino (kind of wool); 'me' + 'RI' (Rhode Island) + 'no' (number)

23 donkey (ass); 'don' (fellow) with 'key' (winding device)

Down

1 dago (South European); 'do' (ditto) + 'ag' (silver)

2 lamplight (artificial illumination); 'l' (left) + 'am' with 'plight' (dilemma)

3 caress (loving touch); 'care' to 'ss' (the ship)

4 powers (strong nations); made by putting 'we' between 'PO' (Post Office) and 'RS' (Royal Society)

5 sty (hog's home); 'st' (little way) with 'y' (yak's head)

6 brethren (brothers); 'BR' (train network) takes 'E' (direction) + 'then' going round 'R' (king)

11 revolting (rebelling); 're' (about) + 'volt' (electric unit) + 'in' + 'g' (gravity)

13 twaddler (senseless talker); 'TWA' (airline) taking 'DD' (divine) to 'le' (the French) 'R' (king)

16 red hot (intensely fiery); 'red' (revolutionary) takes 'O' (nothing) *in* 'HT' (high tension)

17 amends (puts matters right); as 'am' (morning) 'ends' (finishes)

20 shed (cast off); 'she' + ''d' (would, written shortly)

21 gin (spirit); 'GI' (US soldier) goes to 'N' (North)

TEST WORD No. 9 (page 51)

Across

1 ace (one); 'a' + 'C' (hundred) + 'E' (note)

3   private (confidential); 'prate' (prattle) *about* 'iv' (tea-time) =pr–iv–ate

6   leaving (going); 'l' (fifty) to 'ea' (each) +'vi' (six) makes most of it, thus: l–ea–vi–ng

7   lasso (rope noose); 'lass' (girl) with 'o' (nothing) makes it

8   adopt (take responsibility for); 'a' +'D' (500 =crowd) +'opt' (to choose) =a–D–opt

11   Mecca (Islamic city); 'A' +'M' (thousand) +'CC' (two hundred) +'E' (point) *madly* [i.e., anagram] = M–E–CC–a

14   Linda (she); 'Li' (fifty-one) +'N' (north) +'D' (500) + 'a' (note) =Li–N–Da

15   trivial (of little importance); 'iv' (four) *in* 'trial' (test)

16   Cheroot (something to smoke); 'other CO' *ordered* [anag.]

17   see (look at) (bishop's office)

Down

1   acclaim (applause); starts with 'aCC' (a couple of hundred), ends with 'M' (a thousand)

2   elastic (flexible); 'E' (point) to 'last' +'i' (one) +'c' (century)

3   phlox (garden bloomer); 'x' (ten) makes end of it

4   vivid (brilliant); 'vi' (six) +'vi' (six) +'d' (died)

5   erg (work unit); 'Reg' *baffled* [i.e., anag.]

9   oranges (fruit); 'o' (no or none) +'ranges' (mountains)

10   tenable (can be held); 'able' (skilful) after 'ten'

12   cover (lid); 'c' (hundred) +'over' (done with)

13   allot (apportion); 'a' +'L' (fifty) +'lot'

15   tic (twitch); 't' (short time) +'ic' (in charge of)

TEST Word No. 10 (page 52)

Across

1   Hundred years' war (century of fighting); anag. of 'ways harder under'

7   aster (bloomer); *in* pa's territory

8   India (far country); 'in' +'D' (500) +'i' (one) +'a'

10   nun (holy woman)

11   pierces (breaks through); 'r' (king) and 'pieces'

13 ado (fuss); AD–o (year zero)
14 all in (utterly exhausted) (everyone included)
15 oppressor (tyrant); 'op–or' (upset 'poor') *about* 'press' (printing machine)
16 occipital (skull bone); fractured 'I clip coat' [anag.]
18 bless (glorify); 'Bess' (good queen) swallowed 'l' (pound)
20 Dai (Welsh man); 'aid' (help) mixed
21 yoghurt (fermented milk product); made *of* 'thug Roy'
23 ski (mountain 'slipper' – over snow); in 'his kid'
24 get on (go aboard) (make progress)
26 gipsy (Romany); 'GI' (American soldier) takes 'psy' (awkward spy)
28 early closing day (when it's wise to shop before lunch)
Down
 1 having a good time (enjoying oneself); 'avoiding hot game' *madly* [anag.]
 2 rut (groove); *in* 'truth'
 3 dirge (lament); 'G' (German capital) inside 'dir–e'
 4 episcopal (of bishops); 'episc' (odd 'spice') and 'opal' (precious stone)
 5 rid (free); *from* 'pride'
 6 retrogressively (how to go backwards)
 7 annul (cancel); 'what Ann ultimately' holds the word
 9 amass (accumulate) (a large lump)
11 panoply (brilliant array); of 'Pan' (Arcadian god)+ 'O' (making appeal)+'ply' (to work)
12 sherbet (effervescent powder); from 'herb' in 'set'
15 octagonal (eight-sided); 'coal got an' order [anag.]
17 cling (stick together); 'C' (100, or lots of)+'ling' (fish)
19 essay (attempt) (a literary composition)
22 urges (eggs on); *in* 'splurge Sam'
25 try (make an effort) (to irritate)
27 pin (to fix); 'p' (quietly)+'i'+'N' (pole)

TEST Word No. 11 (page 58)

Across
 6 wistful (longing); embroil 'istF' (fist) *with* 'W'+'U'+'L' thus: W(istF)UL

7 delay (put off); 'ye lad' in a flummox [anag.]

9 tunnel (burrow); 'n' (name) in 'tune' (air) to 'L' (novice)

10 images (pictures); 'ie-S' (that is–Southern) has *in* it 'mag' (journal) thus: i(mag)e-S

11 mastication (chewing) 'astic' (I cast badly) 'at–i' (at one) all *in* 'Mon' (county), thus: M(astic–at–i)on

13 elaboration (embroidery); *in* 'elation' (exaltation) 'AB' (sailor) has 'or' (alternative), thus: el(ABor)ation

17 indigo (blue); 'ind' (din shattered)+'I'+'go'

18 easily (without difficulty); 'ea' (each)+'i' (one) put *in* 'sly' surroundings, thus: ea–s(i)ly

19 unwed (unmarried); *in* 'fun we d*elight'

20 custody (imprisonment); 'Cody' (Buffalo Bill) taking *in* 'U' (Upperclass) 'st' (saint), thus: C(U–st)ody

Down

1 minus (without); 'M' (Monsieur)+'in'+(US)

2 stanza (verse); 'sta' (sat awkwardly)+'Z' (last letter) *in* 'NA' (North America), thus: sta–N(z)A

3 bullet-proof (slug resistant); order 'full probe to' [anag.] become it

4 depart (leave) 'de–art' (haphazard trade) about 'p'

5 page boy ('Buttons'); 'g' (note)+'EBO' (troubled OBE or Honour) in 'pay', thus: pa(g+EBO)y

8 discotheque (where records spin); 'Di's'+'co' join 'the' +'que' (shortened queue), this: Dis–co–the–que

12 planing (soaring); 'p' (quietly)+'lag' (old convict) taking *in* 'nin' (ruined inn or pub), thus: p–la(nin)g

14 boiled (heightened temperature); 'o' (ring) 'il' (the Italian) *in* 'bed' (or resting), thus: b(o–il)ed

15 onsets (attacks); 'nset' (sent astray) in 'OS' (outsize)

16 glide (glance, cricket stroke) 'l' (left) *in* 'Gide' (writer)

TEST WORD No. 12 (page 64)

Across

6 stroke (paralytic attack); 'KO' reversal in it

7 Chopin (the composer); 'pin' finally is 'nip' *back*

8 investigation (research into); 'inves' (tangled 'vines')
   +ti–gat–i–on ('no, I tag it' *back*)
9 droop (wilt); D (500, or crowd)+'roop' (poor returning)
10 Anna (her, each way) also old Indian coin
11 path (walker's way); 'pat' ('tap' *back*)+'h' (hard)
14 peels (strips); also 'sleep' (slumber) *returning*
16 probabilities (likelihoods); anag. of 'alibi, it probes'
18 billed (advertised); 'bil' (Lib come-back)+'led' (went
   ahead)
19 noodle (one in the soup); 'no' ('on' reflection)+anag. of
   'dole'

Down

1 atoned (made restitution); 'a'+'ton' ('not' *up*)+'ed'
2 come to the ball (invitation to the dance)
3 meet (hunt gathering); 'teem' (or pour) *upwards*
4 contravention (infringement); 'convention' (a fashion)
   holding 'tra' (art *up*)
5 disown (cut off); dis (Sid somersaulting)+anag. of
   'now'
7 cigar (havanna); CI+'gar' (rag *up*)
12 afraid (scared); 'a'+'f' (loud)+'raid' (incursion)
13 tubed (went by Underground); ='debut' (launching)
   upwards
15 steely (coldly hard); 'leet' turning *up* in 'Sy' (Surrey)
17 line (rank); 'E' (the East, or Orient) props *up* 'nil'

TEST WORD No. 13 (page 65)

Across

1 mini-skirt; (a hem short in the 1970s)
5 cabal (secret clique); 'BA' in 'Cal' (California)
8 sag (droop); 'gas' back
9 nest egg (something laid up), for the future
11 sou (very little money/coin); 'so'+'U' (what's 'done')
12 Clive (him); in 'Stoi*c Lives*'
14 Orleans, where Joan of Arc, 'Maid of Orleans' was
   first regarded by the English as a witch
16 Lerwick (Scottish town); anag. of 'to kill crew' *without*
   L–o–t

18 variety (mixture) (mixed entertainment)
20 andiron (fire-dog); 'and' (also)+'iron' (golf club)
22 ingot (metal mass); 'got in' transposed
24 ass (fool); of 'a'+'ss' (ship
25 andante (slow movement – music.) 'Dan' enters 'ante'
27 awl (boring instrument); 'law' muddled
28 Mecca (holy city); anag. of C-came
30 aerated (charged with gas and air)
32 do or die (desperate alternatives); hidden words
33 eagerly (keenly); 'ge' ('e.g.' turning) in 'early'

Down

1 musically (harmoniously); 'mus' (sum *up*)+'ic'+'ally'
2 nag (scold) (the horse)
3 singe (scorch); 'ing' (mixed gin) in 'SE'
4 in stock (available); hidden words
5 cog (wheel tooth); 'o' (nothing) in 'c.g.'
6 basis (fundamental ingredient); 'bass' swallows 'i'
7 laundry (washing); anag. of 'lady run'
10 enliven (animate); hidden word
13 inroads (incursions)
15 air line (traffic system)
17 Indiana (in US); 'an' (article) in 'India'
19 England (part of UK); 'and' follows anag. of 'glen'
21 red tape (colourful binding); can hold everything up
23 tallboy (long fellow) (chest of drawers)
24 aimed (directed); 'me' in 'aid'
26 nurse (foster) (sister, possibly)
29 coo (dovelike sound); often hear 'Bill and Coo'
31 tug (pull); 'gut' (violin string) when read upwards

TEST WORD No. 14 (page 71)

Across

1 lynx (animal); sounds like 'links' (golf)
5 seas (oceans); utterly 'seize' (appropriate)
7 raiment (clothing); we hear 'ray meant' (intended)
8 prey (victim); 'tis said 'pray' (may do so on knees)
10 tee (drive off-point) (golf); sounds like 'tea'

11   pane (window glass); pronouncedly can give 'pain'

13   scorer (winner of points); 'sr' (senior) takes 'core' (heart) to heart, thus: s(core)r

15   twenty (a score); for five 'sets of four'=20

17   muddle (mess); 'DD' (theologian) *in* 'mule' (slipper)

19   Cretan (of Crete, Gk island); kind of 'trance' [anag.]

20   Otto ('he'); makes 'to' go backwards *and* forwards

22   Eve ('she'); reads the same whether to or fro

23   when (say 'when!') if there's enough in the glass

25   sighted (can see); audibly 'sited'

26   sale (the selling); sound 'sail' (canvas sheet)

27   erne (bird, eagle); we say 'earn' (merit pay)

Down

1   lisp (utter with imperfection); at letter 's' (19th)

2   X-ray (photograph); shows what can't be otherwise seen

3   filter (strain); a 'philtre' as they say

4   decent (modest); 'descent' without 's' (old Bob, or shilling)

5   step (tread); Russian 'steppe', we hear

6   site (place); heard in 'sighted-sited'

9   racquet (stringed implement); does it make racket (din)?

12   nitrate (chemical); sounds like 'night rate'

14   red (colour); soundly 'read' (perused)

16   ewe (sheep); 'you' echo

18   emerge (reappear); from '. . . d*e mer ge*nteelly' (hidden)

19   cheats (frauds); 'c' (century)+'heats' (warms)

20   ours (belong to us); 'hours', 'tis said

21   Ouse (river); pronounced 'ooze' (slimy mud)

23   wade (walk through water); utterly 'weighed'

24   nose (sniffer); sounds like 'knows' (knowledgeable)

TEST WORD No. 15 (page 76)

Across

1   spring (bound); no 'hands' (workers)

4   ramp (slope); 'Ted' lost

8   Maman (French Mum); madman drops 'd' (penny of old)

9   ozone (lusty air); anag. of (d)ozen–o(peras), no 'drapes'

10   instalment (part of serial); 'l' (pound)+'me' in 'instant'

12   convergent (meeting); without 'erg' leaves 'convent'

16   overt (public); 'Ure' (river, or flow–er) cut from over-ture

17   agate (quartz); hidden word

18   lies (replies falsely); no 'rep' (material) in 'replies'

19   leased (let); no 'p' ('soft' head) in 'pleased'

Down

1   sump (pit); chuck 'us out' from 'sumptuous'

2   Roman (Italian); no 'C.E.' in 'romance'

3   nineteenth (last century) (golfer's easiest 'hole')

5   alone (solitary); no 'M' in 'alone'

6   pretty (attractive); 'TT' added to 'prey'

7   collegiate (like a college); anag. of 'Galileo, etc.'

11   school (mostly 'cool'); prefix of 'masters'

13   niece (relative); anag. of 'nice tea' without 'ta'

14   nears (approaches); anag. of 'answers' without 'SW'

15   pend (hang in balance); 'Pendragon' with no rag on

TEST WORD No. 16 (page 77)

Across

1   sailing (at sea); 's' –ailing

4   get well (obtain water supply) (to be cured)

7   lupin (a bloomer); L–up–in

9   leakage (escape) (news leakage)

11   Ted (make hay) (boy)

13   oppidan (college non-resident); anag. of pop–in–ad

15   boa (snake) (coil of feathers)

17   shortly (briefly); 'hort' enclosed by 'sly'

19   nerve; bold shows nerve, scared show nerves

20   sprayed (sprinkled); 'sped' round 'ray'

22   let-down (disappointment); short dress might be

24   today (at this date); 'toady' (fawner) with inside twisted

26   clipper (sailing craft); anag. of 'cripple'

28   mac (rainwear); 'tar' (jack) has gone

30 cringed (cowered); hidden word
32 Ure (river); anag. of 'rue'
33 split peas (dried veg); anag. of 'it's apples'
34 widen (expand); W.I.–den

Down

1 split (divide) (rent)
2 imp (wicked spirit); i–MP
3 galipot (turpentine); anag. of 'got a lip'
4 grand (magnificent); possibly grandparents
5 tea (meal); anag. of 'ate'
6 luggage (bags) (trunks)
8 neology (new word-meanings); anag., of 'go on Ely'
10 embargo (ban); 'MBA' in 'ergo'
12 desired (wanted); anag. of 'side' over 'der' upwards
14 non-stop (uninterrupted); French 'non'+'stop'
16 fast times (high speeds) (periods of abstinence)
18 yelling (howling); Y–el–ling
21 deceive (mislead); 'C' in 'Dee'+I've
23 nankeen (material or stuff); makes Nan+keen
25 yacht (sailing craft)
27 round (ring); hidden word
29 col (mountain pass)
31 dew (early freshness); 'we'd' read upwards

TEST WORD No. 17 (page 81)

Across

1 up the pole (where flag is) (in a fix) (up North)
5 crate (case); for 'ape' travelling by 'plane'
8 den (lair); 'Ned' backwards
9 haughty (uppish); ha–(ught)–y
11 ape (imitate) (primate)
12 rider
14 eclipse
16 assault (attack); hidden word
18 drawing (magnetic) (sketch)
20 acidity (sourness); hidden word
22 impel (urge); i–MP–el
24 pad (stuff); for drawing on

25   outcast (thrown off)
27   old (of such age)
28   adorn (bedeck); ado–RN
30   Neptune
32   embrace (hug); E–MB–RAC–E
33   nonplus (puzzle); 'non'+'plus' French

Down

1   undertake (pledge) (conduct a funeral)
2   tan (brown); on holiday, maybe
3   ether
4   opulent (rich); op–U–Lent
5   coy (small company) (rather shy)
6   amaze (astonish) (a labyrinth)
7   evening
10   holiday (a break); in Neptune's company?
13   discard (throw away); dis (Sid upwards)+card
15   pianist
17   unicorn (one-horned); anag. of 'I con NUR'
19   implore (entreat); imp–lore
21   intense (emotional); anag. of 'in teens'
23   lodgers (boarding-house dwellers); on holiday?
24   plane (a Trident, perhaps); unlike Neptune's
26   aspen
29   orb (eye); 'bro' backwards
31   urn (vase); we hear 'earn'

TEST WORD No. 18 (page 88)

Across

1   divided and ruled
7   Magog
8   civic (same both ways)
10   lex (Roman law); hidden word
11   Knossos (where Minotaur was in labyrinth)
13   bin (wine holder)
14   beret
15   whitewash (cover-up) (washing pegged out)
16   residency (home of His Excellency)
18   Padua; pad–U–a

20 ear
21 Detroit (centre of Fords); de–T(roi)T
23 nil (nothing); 'in' back+L
24 monks (monastics) (bullfinches)
26 issue (outcome); is–Sue
28 disentanglement (undoing)

Down

1 double-barrelled (kind of surname) (kind of shotgun)
2 dog (shadow) (hound)
3 doggo (to lie doggo)
4 necessity ('mother of invention')
5 rev (little reverend); part of 'rev–olutionary'
6 disenthrallment (freedom from bondage); anag.
7 mixer
9 cobra (snake); anag. of 'crab'+'o'
11 Katydid (type of grasshopper); anag.
12 stewpot
15 went to sea (went to see)
17 scrum (scrimmage); sc–rum
19 Dante (Italian poet); d–ante
22 owing (in debt); no 'cr'
25 non (turn-down); French 'no'
27 Sue (girl) (go to court)

TEST WORD No. 19 (page 92)

Across

1 backing horses (gee-gees spelt backwards)
6 one over the eight
13 are (exist); hidden word
15 adhesion
16 rovers; 'r'–over–'s'
17 & 25 parallel bars
20 drawback (snag); 'draw' written *back*wards
21 endear; anag. of 'neared'
22 chillier (colder); chilli–ER
24 Lib (party); (ad.)LIB.(ber)
26 electrification
33 love and kisses

Down

1 bon; repeated, would make bonbon
2 kava (Polynesian drink); k+Ava
3 got (obtained); hidden word
4 ore; o+RE
5 soh
6 over and done
7 eras (ages); anag.
8 red (coloured)
9 heehaw
10 Elijah
11 gentlemen
12 triple crown
14 avalanche
18 oboist; anag.
19 ocelli (eyelike colour spots); anag.
21 Eric; heather, or erica, shortened
23 Eli; anag. of 'lie'
25 see 17
27 Lil; anag. of 'ill'
28 RIA
29 fad (craze); hidden word
30 ops

TEST WORD No. 20 (page 94)

Across 1 the back of beyond; 9 W–oo; 10 die-hard;
11 bus; 12 rider; 14 ill; 15 drier; 17 Feb–rile; 19 yield
up; 21 Titanic; 23 stimuli; 24 end up; 26 awl; 27 mitre;
28 get; 30 lie down; 31 hoe; 32 horticulturists.
Down 1 tower of strength; 2 ego; 3 adder; 4 K–he–dive;
5 frailty; 6 ended; 7 orb; 8 descriptiveness; 13 de–bit–ed;
16 in DouBt; 18 Ian; 20 El–I; 22 chat–eau; 23 sold out
(sole doubt); 25 pal–pi; 27 manor; 29 tar; 31 HMS.

TEST WORD No. 21 (page 96)

Across

1 printing presses
7 ca–PO–n
8 uvula
10 eg–o
11 not done
13 ant
14 dinner set
16 sting
17 cacti
19 x–eroder–ma (hidden)
21 la–x
22 given up
24 ash
25 Dover
27 T–em–p–T
29 you never can tell

Down

1 Perpendicularly
2 tip
3 ninety-six
4 Pluto (plutôt)
5 emu
6 stratigraphical
7 c–low–n
9 abaci
11 needing
12 eased up
15 threnetic
18 co–x–ed
20 re–act
23 verse
26 vie
28 man

Glossary

The following is a collection of terms which are frequently found in cryptic crossword clues, and with which experienced solvers will be already familiar. In no way should the glossary be regarded as either a dictionary or as a comprehensive collection of synonyms, nor should any of the suggested interpretations be regarded as binding. This is intended solely to be a guide to help beginners to find possible leads in cryptic clues.

A

Abbess, Abbey, Abbot: abb

Aboard, on board: possibly a letter, or group of letters, between letters 's.s.' (steamship) implying being in a ship (e.g., 'tar aboard . . .' could give 'stars')

About: re, concerning *or* possibly an anagram, the letters being moved *about* (e.g., 'leaps about . . .' could give 'sepal', 'pales' or 'peals'); *or*, in maritime context, letters being reversed; *or* could indicate that one word is written round, or *about*, another (e.g., 'sing about now . . .' could give 's(now)ing')

Abstainer: TT

Academician: RA, ARA

Acceptable: OK, U

Accolade: see under 'honours' and 'title'

Account: ac, acc, bill; tale, story

Accountant: CA

Achieve: do, get, attain

Add, addition: sum; PS *or* possibly letters or word added to another

Address, -es, -ing: O, Oh

Admiral: adm

Adrift: might indicate an anagram, the spelling *drifting* into other form (e.g., 'vessel adrift . . .' could give 'selves')

Advertisement: ad, advert

Afloat: possibly as 'aboard' (above), enclosed by 's.s.'

Afresh: might indicate an anagram, letters being arranged *afresh* (e.g., 'sung afresh . . .' could give 'snug', 'guns', or 'gnus')

Africa, South: SA

African River: Nile, Congo

Afternoon: pm (in the afternoon)

Afterthought, -s: PS, PPS

Again: bis, ditto, do

Against: (versus) v; anti, no, noes *or*, if 'up against', perhaps one word or syllable against, or joining, another

Agent: agt, rep, spy

Agree, -s, -ing: nod, nods, nodding, assents, concurs

Aide, aide de camp: ADC

Air: mien; tune, melody

Air force, Air power: RAF; (former, old) RFC

Airline: BA, BEA, BOAC, SAS, PanAm, ELAL, TWA, etc.

Air man: FO, PO, pilot, flier

Alcohol: gin, rum, brandy, nip, tot (see also under *Wine*)

Alderman: ald

All over the place: possibly an anagram, the spelling being *all over the place* (e.g., 'streams all over the place . . .' could give 'masters')

Allow: let

Alpha: a

All right, alright: OK, U

Altered: might indicate an anagram, a word's letters being *altered* (e.g., 'altered room . . .' gives 'moor')

Alternative, -ly: or

Aluminium: al

Amateur: A, L (learner), tyro; (radio) ham

Ambassador: HE

America: US

American: Am, Yank, Yankee; (Uncle) Sam; (-soldier) GI; lawyer (Dist. Attorney) DA

Amidships: see 'aboard' and 'afloat'

Amok: may indicate an anagram, the letters *running amok* (e.g., 'slaves running amok . . .' could give 'salves')

Amputated: could indicate a letter or syllable has been cut off, or amputated, from a word

Ancient: possibly old or obsolete word or spelling (e.g., 'your ancient . . .' could be 'thy'; 'ancient appeal' might be 'prithee')

Ancient city: Ur

Anew: might indicate an anagram (e.g., 'read anew' gives 'dear' or 'dare')

Anger: rage, ire, fury

Angry: raging, ranting; *or* possibly denotes an anagram (e.g., 'angry words . . .' gives 'sword')

Animal: those most often seen in crossword puzzles include: ape, ass, bear, boar, bull, camel, cat, cow, cur, deer, doe, dog, eland, elk, ewe, foal, fox, goat, gnu, hare, hog, horse, lion, lynx, mare, mice, mole, mouse, mule, ox, oxen, panda, pig, pony, pug, puma, pup, rat, ram, rhino, seal, sow, stag, stoat, teg, tiger, tup, wolf, yak

Announcement: ad, advert

Answer: ans, reply

Antelope: eland

Appeal, -ing: O! Oh!

Appendix: app, PS

April: Apr, Apl

Arbiter: ref

Architect, -ure: arch, (Body) RIBA

Army: (territorial) TA, (Salvation) SA

Around: may indicate an anagram, letters being shuffled *around* (e.g., 'wrote around' gives 'tower') *or* may indicate that one group of letters is 'around' another (e.g., 'pig around pin' would give 'piping')

Arrange, -ed, -ing: arr; *or* might indicate an anagram, letters being *arranged* (e.g., 'letters arranged' could give 'trestle')

Arrive, -al, -ed: arr

Arsenic: as

Article: a, an, etc.
(French article) un, une, etc. (German article) ein

Artillery: RA, guns, cannon

Artist: (usually 'famous') RA, ARA, PRA *or* possibly the name of a painter. Those seen most frequently in crosswords include: Hals, Lely, Lowry, Manet, Monet, Orpen, Renoir, Rubens, Spencer, Turner, Whistler

Ass: fool, dope, dupe, lout, oaf, sop, sap

Assent, give assent: nod, nods, yes, aye

Assistance: aid, help

Assemble, -ed, -bly: possibly an anagram, the letters being *assembled* differently (e.g., 'assembled stars' could give 'Tsars')

Associate: ally, pal

Association: Ass., assoc.

Atomic: A (A-bomb)

Attorney (District): DA

August: Aug

Aunt: possibly Sally

Austere: Spartan, ascetic

Avenue: av, ave

Away: out, gone off

Awkward, awkwardly: could indicate an anagram (e.g., 'Limped awkwardly' gives 'dimple')

Awry: similarly to 'awkwardly', might indicate an anagram

B

Back, backwards, comes back: often indicates that a group of letters is spelt backwards. (e.g., 'Meg, coming back . . .' gives 'gem')

Bachelor: BA (Bachelor of Arts), MB (Bachelor of Medicine), etc.

Bad, badly: possibly denotes an anagram, letters being arranged *badly* (e.g., 'Plums badly . . .' or 'Bad plums . . .' could give 'slump')

Baronet: bt, bart

Battalion: Bn

Batter, -ed, -ing: might suggest an anagram, the word being *battered* into a different shape (e.g., 'Battering rams' could give 'arms' or 'Mars')

Bear, -ing, -s: in a *down* clue, could indicate one word holding or carrying (i.e., bearing), another above it

Bed: cot *In* bed, might refer to plants in a garden bed (e.g., 'girl in a bed . . .' could be 'Rose')

Bed and breakfast: bb

Beginner: L (learner), tyro, novice

Behead, -ing, -s, -ed: probably refers to a word being beheaded by having its first letter cut off (e.g., 'tramp beheaded . . .' would give 'ramp')

Behold: Lo! see!

Bird: those most frequently appearing in crossword puzzles are: auk, cock, coot, crane, crow, daw, diver, dodo, dove, duck, eagle, egret, eider, emu, erne, finch, fowl, geese, goose, gull, hawk, hen, heron, ibis, jay, kite, kiwi, lark, magpie, mew, mina, myna, owl, pie, pipit, raven, robin, roc, rook, snipe, stork, swan, teal, tern, thrush, tit, wader, wren

Bizarre: odd *or* might suggest an anagram or *bizarre* spelling alternative (i.e., 'bizarre features . . .' could give 'safe, true')

Black (pencils): b, bb

Bloomer: error *or* possibly a flower, i.e., something that blooms (see list under 'flower')

Blown up: possibly indicates an anagram, the spelling being *blown up* into something different (e.g., 'big red blown up . . .' could give 'bridge')

Bluff: might refer to a promontory, geographically; *or*, with King or Monarch, to Hal

Blushing: red, rosy

Board: table *or* possibly company, co, *or* aboard ship, when see under 'aboard'

Boat: see 'ship'

Bob, old: s (shilling in old currency)

Bombardier: bdr

Book: tome, vol; order, enter

Border: edge, rim, hem, haha (sunken fence)

Bore: drill

Born: b, ne, nee

Boss: stud

Bother: ado, fuss

Both ways (going, looking): possibly a palindrome, or word which reads the same backwards or forwards (e.g., 'flatten both ways' could be 'level')

Bowled: b

Bowling spell (cricket): over

Boy: he, lad, son *or* possibly boy's name, maybe in shortened form (see list under 'names')

Brave man: VC, MC, DSC, DSM, DFC, DFM, etc.; hero

Break, -ing, broken: could refer to an anagram (e.g., 'broken line' could give 'Neil')

Britain: GB, UK, Brit

British: Brit

Broadcasting: BBC; spreading, sewing

Broken, brokenly: see under 'break'

Brother: br, bro, fra, friar

Brown: tan

Bumkin, bumpkin: ass, fool, oaf, lout, dope

Buckled: might indicate an anagram, the spelling being *buckled* into different shape (e.g., 'buckled panel . . .' could give 'plane')

Burst, busted: possibly means an anagram (e.g., 'burst eardrum' could give 'a murder')

Butter: might be an animal that 'butts', e.g., a goat or ram, *or* a person who says 'but . . .'. or 'yet . . .'

C

Call: ring (phone); bid; hi!

Capital: possibly the capital letter beginning a proper noun (e.g., 'Martin's capital'='M') *or* a capital city, usually Oslo, Paris, Rome, etc. *or*, for Capital people, Parisians, Romans, etc.

Caps: in a *down* clue, might indicate that one group of letters 'caps', or stands above, another (e.g., 'he caps a postscript' could mean that 'he' stands on top of 'a PS' giving 'heaps')

Captive: pow (prisoner of war) *or* possibly means one group of letters holds another captive (e.g., 'Mary holding son captive' would give 'ma–son–ry')

Carbon: c

Carry, carries: in *down* clue, might mean a lower group of letters holds up, or carries, an upper one

Catch: net, trap, snag

Cathedral city: frequently Ely or York

Caught: c

Caught up, up in: may indicate an anagram (e.g., 'robe caught up . . .' could give 'bore') *or* may mean that one word is 'caught up' within another, especially in a *down* clue (see 'captive')

Celebration: do, fete

Centigrade: c

Ceremony, ceremonies: (master of) MC

Certain: sure

Change, -d, -s, -ing: may refer to an anagram (e.g., 'changing plans' could give 'N. Alps')

Channel, across the: possibly indicates a French word or syllable

Channel Isles: CI

Chaos, chaotic, -ally: probably infers an anagram, or *chaotic* spelling (e.g., 'boardroom in a state of chaos' could give 'Broadmoor')

Charge, in charge of, man in charge: ic, co, boss

Child: possibly son, tot, nipper, etc.

Christopher: Kit

Church: ch, kirk

Church of England: CE

Church, Roman: RC

Churchman: rev., DD, dean, curate, rector, Abbe, abbot, prior, cure, Father, Fr, parson, minister

Circle: o, ring, round

Citizen (senior): OAP

City: (ancient) Ur
(cathedral) Ely, York

Civil Defence: CD ARP (air raid precautions)

Civil Engineer: CE

Clamour: din, row, noise

Clasp: might be one word written around, or *clasping*, another (e.g., 'Ted clasping Ann' would give 'tanned')

Class: (first class or top class) Ai, Al, A; (second class) B; (third class) C; (upper class) U

Classic: might refer to racing event, e.g., 'Oaks' *or* to Latin word (e.g., 'classic law . . .' might be 'lex')

Classical: possibly relating to ancient Greece, history or buildings, mythology, etc.

Clergyman: see under 'churchman'

Climb, -s, -ing: possibly refers to a word read or climbing upwards, in a *down* solution

Clothing: gear

Club: (golf) iron; (cricket) MCC; (motoring) RAC

Clumsy, -ily: may indicate an anagram (e.g., 'clumsily grip pint' could give 'tripping')

Cockney: maybe a word which has the Cockney *sound* of another one, possibly dropped aitch, etc. (e.g., 'Cockney heater' could be 'eater')

Coin: p; bob or s (shilling in 'old' or former currency); d (old penny); crown (old)
or possibly a foreign coin. Those most frequently used in crossword puzzles are: anna, cent, dime, ducat, ecu, franc, lira, lire, louis, mark, peso, real, rouble, rupee, sen, sou, yen

Cold: c, b-r-r, icy

Collapse, -s, -d, -ing: possibly indicates an anagram, where word structure has *collapsed* into something else (e.g., 'collapsed arches' could give 'search')

College: very often Eton; possibly coll; could be Kings, Girton, etc.

Colonel: col

Colour, -s: flag, standard; hue, shade, tone; *or* amber, beige, blue, brown, caramel, fawn, grey, green, lime, mauve, pink, purple, red, sage, scarlet, sienna, red, tan, violet, etc.

Colourless: ashen, pale, wan

Column: col

Comes back to: possibly one group of letters *read backwards* adjoining another (e.g., 'cat comes back to it' would give 'tacit')

Comes to: one word joining another – or their synonyms (i.e., 'doctor comes to ill' would give 'drill')

Comes up to: in a *down* clue, might refer to how a group of letters might read from bottom upwards

Commanding Officer: CO

Common, commonly: may refer to a word or pronunciation as 'commonly' used, either by dropped aitch or perhaps by popular, or common, slang or figure of speech (e.g. 'common prison' could be 'jug', 'quod', 'stir', etc.) *or* could refer to name of a Common, such as Clapham, Tooting, etc.

Communist: comm, red

Companion: mate; (of Honour) CH

Company: co, coy, set

Complicate, -d, -s: might indicate an anagram, a spelling having been *complicated* into another (e.g., 'complicated sewing' could give 'swinge')

Conceal, -ed, -ing, -ment, -s: could indicate that a group of letters or word *conceals* another within it (e.g., 'detractor concealing pamphlet' would conceal 'tract')

Concerning: re, about

Concludes, conclusion: probably refers to the last letter or syllable of a word (e.g., conclusion of 'perambulate' could be 'ate' or 'late')

Concoction: may indicate an anagram, a new word having been *concocted* from another (e.g., 'hot fry concoction' could give 'frothy')

Confused, confusion: may indicate an anagram of *confused* letters (e.g., 'confused cheater . . .' could give 'teacher')

Conservative: con, Tory

Constabulary: force

Contain, -ed, -ing, -s: may indicate that a group of letters or word is *contained* within another (e.g., 'River [Ure] is contained by ten' would give 'tureen')

Continents: Europe, Asia, Africa, Australia, America

Contort, -ed, -ing, -s: might indicate an anagram, a word being *contorted* into another (e.g., 'contorted spine' could give 'snipe')

Converse: could denote the opposite of a given word (e.g., 'loud converse' could mean 'quiet', 'genteel', etc.)

Copper: Cu, bobbie (policeman)
'old' copper: d (pre-decimal penny)

Corporal: cpl

Cot: bed

Country: Those occurring most frequently in crossword puzzles include: Alaska, Arabia, Britain, Burma, Canada, Chile, China, Cuba, Eire, France, Gambia, GB, Greece, India, Iran, Italy, Japan, Kenya, Korea, Libya, Malaya, Monaco, Panama, Persia, Peru, Poland, Russia, Sicily, Spain, Sweden, Sudan, Tibet, Tobago, Tonga, Uganda, UK, US, USSR, Wales, Zaire, Zambia

County: Co.; English counties no longer existing since the boundaries were redrawn may be referred to as 'old' or 'former' counties. Abbreviations of counties frequently seen in crossword puzzles are: Beds, Berks, Bucks, Bute, Caern, Carm, Ches, Derbys, Devon, Essex, Fife, Flint, Glam, Glos, Hants, Herts, Hunts, Kent, Lancs, Leics, Lincs, Mddx, Mon, Mont, Moray, Nairn, Notts, Pem, Oxon, Ross, Salop Som, Sx, Sy, Warks, Wilts, Worcs, Yorks.
New counties in England and Wales since 1 April 1974 include: Avon, Cleveland, Clwyd, Cumbria, Dyfed, Gwent, Gwynedd, Humberside, Powys. New metropolitan counties: Greater Manchester, Merseyside, Tyne & Wear, West Midlands, South Yorks, West Yorks.

Couple: pair, pr, two

Court: woo

Craft: possibly skill, e.g., art, pottery *or* possibly boat or ship, punt, canoe, etc.

Craftsman: possibly a skilled worker *or* one engaged in rowing or sailing a boat

Crazy: could denote an anagram (e.g., 'crazy boardroom . . .' could give 'Broadmoor')

Creature: often turns out to be an 'eft'

Crew: eight

Cricket: (body) MCC

Crooked, -ly: could imply an anagram, a word being spelt *crookedly* (e.g., 'crooked trade . . .' could give 'tread' or 'rated')

Cross: x

Crowd: mob, mass *or* a roman figure for a large number (e.g., D for five hundred, M for a thousand, etc.)

Cupid: Eros

Currency: p (pence); l (pound); dollar; frank; mark; see also under 'coins'

Current: now; AC, DC, *or* might indicate a river, or flowing water

Curious, -ly: could indicate an anagram, the letters being arranged in a *curious* way (e.g., 'spied lady curiously' could give 'displayed')

Curtailed: probably a word having its last letter or syllable cut off (e.g. 'Curtailed ration . . .' gives 'ratio')

Custom: use, usage

Cut: see 'curtailed'

Cypher, royal: ER

D

Dandy: beau, fop

Daughter: dtr

Day: see 'weekday'

Dead: d, dec, late

Debtor: dr

Debts: I.O.U.S.

December: Dec

Decorations: VC, MC, MM, DFC, DFM, etc.

Defence: CD, ARP

Degree: probably academic ,e.g., BA, BSc, MA, DD, etc. *or* deg

Denomination: CE, RC

Department: dept

Design, -ed, -s: Probably denotes an anagram, a word being *designed* into another spelling (e.g., 'designed tower' could give 'wrote')

Detectives: CID

Devil: Satan, Lucifer, demon; (little) imp

Difficult, in difficulties: may denote an anagram, the spelling being *in difficulties* (e.g., 'Amy chants in difficulties' could give 'yachtsman')

Different, -ly: might indicate an anagram, the arrangement of letters being *different* (e.g., 'different being' could make 'begin')

Diminutive: probably an abbreviated noun or a shortened Christian name. See also under 'little'

Direction: (in movement) l (left), r (right), bk (backwards), to and fro, *or* points of compass, N, S, E, W, NE SW, SE, NW

Directors, -s, of company: dir, dirs, board

Disarray, -ed: possibly implies an anagram, the letters being *in disarray* (e.g., 'boss, in disarray' could give 'sobs')

Disc: lp (long playing), ep (extended play)

Disciplined: drilled, trained, Spartan

Disfigure: mar, scar, blot

Disheartened: probably a word has the exactly central letter or letters removed (e.g., 'disheartened Peter' gives 'peer')

Dishevelled; Dispersed; Displaced: possibly indicate an anagram (e.g., 'Hikers, dishevelled . . .' could give 'shrike')

Distance: probably an abbreviated or short measure – in, inch, ft, foot, yd, yard, mile, m, kilo. (See also under 'measure'.)

Distilled, distillation: possibly an anagram implied (e.g., 'distillation of red rum' yields 'murder')

Distort, -ed, -ion, -s: may indicate an anagram (e.g., 'distorted report' could produce 'porter')

District: dist *or* may refer to a metropolitan or postal district, as SE, NE, NW, SW, Cen, EC, WC

District Attorney: DA

Disturbed, disturbance: possibly denotes an anagram, the spelling being *disturbed* (e.g., 'disturbance of shop . . .' can produce 'posh')

Ditto: do

Divinity, Doctor of: DD

Doctor: dr, GP, MO, MD, doc, LlD, DD

Document, -s: deed, deeds, MS, MSS

Dog: cur, pup; *or* breed, such as Corgi, poodle, Peke, terrier; *or* hound, shadow, follow

Doze: nod, kip, sleep, zz

Dozen: doz

Drink: (usually little) nip, tot, pint, pt; (kind) gin, rum, ale, tea, wine, cider, beer, lemonade (see also under 'alcohol' and 'wine')

Driver: motorist, club

Drop off: doze, nod; fall

Drops: may indicate a word *dropping* a letter (e.g., 'peach, dropping quietly . . .' leaves 'each')

Drunk, -en, -enly: may suggest an anagram, the letters *reeling about* (e.g., 'drunken rage . . .' could give 'gear')

Dry: sec
Duck: O
Dutchman: Hans

E

Each: ea
East, Eastern: E
East, Middle: ME
Eastern, or Middle Eastern, potentate, ruler, leader, etc.,:
Emir, Ali, Shah, Aga, Bey, Czar, Mikado
Eccentric: might imply an anagram, letters being arranged in
an *eccentric* way (e.g., 'eccentric earl . . .' could be 'Lear')
Echo: might refer to one word sounding like, or *echoing* another
while being spelt differently (e.g., 'Echo of Time . . .' could
be 'thyme')
Edge: rim, hem, lip
Edition: ed
Editor: ed
Education: learning
Education, Local – Authority: LEA
Effort: essay, try
Egg, -s: (duck's) o, oo
Egyptian goddess: Isis
Eight: crew
Embrace: hug *or* might indicate that one group of letters or
word *embraces* or wraps itself around another (e.g., 'Fred,
embracing own . . .' would give 'frowned')
Emperor: emp
Employer: user, boss
Empty: could be a word with 'o' (nothing) inserted into it (e.g,
'empty cup . . .' could be 'coup')
Enclose: pen, fence *or* might indicate a group of letters being
enclosed by or within another (e.g., 'marsh enclosed in de-
fences' would give 'fen')
Engineer, Civil: CE
Engineers, Royal: RE
England, English: Eng
Ennoble: see under 'title'
Envelop, -ed, -ing, -s: may indicate that one group of letters
envelops another (e.g., 'theologian with the French enveloped
by mud . . .' could give 'muddled', i.e., mu(DD–le)d
Epoch: age, era

Equal, equality: par

Erupter: probably a volcano such as Etna

Erupting: could indicate an anagram, where the letters *erupt* into a different order (e.g., 'Etna erupting . . .' might give the answer 'neat')

Essay: try

Essayist: Elia, Lamb, Pope, etc.

European Organization: EEC

Europeans: those most frequently occurring in crossword puzzles include: Pole, Slav, Swiss, Lett, Lapp, Dane, Swede, Finn, Dago

Even: level

Evening: eve, or possibly ironing

Ex: meaning formerly, see under 'old'

Examination: test, oral

Example: (for) eg; model

Excess: over, too; glut, surplus

Excellency: HE

Exclaim, -s, exclamation: ah aha, fie, bah, bosh, la, lo, my, O, Ooh, Och, Oh, hi, hey, eh, pah, pooh, tut, whew, ugh

Executed: may mean that a word has been decapitated, or lost its first letter or syllable (e.g., 'Parson executed for fire-raising . . .' could give 'arson')

Exercise: (physical) PT

Expert: ace, star, pro, dab

Explode, -d, -ing, -s: might mean an anagram (e.g., 'flails ace explosively . . .' could give 'fallacies')

Explosive: TNT, (high explosive) HE

Extinct (creature): probably relates to 'dodo'

Extraordinary: possibly denotes an anagram (e.g., 'extra-ordinary ideas . . .' could give 'aside')

Extreme, extremity: probably refer to first and/or last letters of a word (e.g., 'passions' extremes . . .' would give 'pans')

Eyesore: usually a stye

F

Fabricate, -d, -ion, -ing, -s: possibly indicates an anagram, the word being *fabricated* into something else (e.g., 'fabricated lies . . .' could give 'isle')

False, -ly: might denote an anagram (e.g., 'Falsely promise . . .' could give 'imposer')

Fates: Atropos, Clotho and Lachesis

Father: Dad, pa, pater, Pop, fr, Fra; sire

Favours, in favour of: pro

Favourite: pet

February: Feb

Fellow: man, boy, chap; (of University), don; (of Society), F; (of Royal Society), FRS, etc. *or* may indicate a male by name (e.g., Fred, Tom) (see also under 'names')

Feminine: f, fem, she, her

Few: possibly written numbers up to ten, or Roman figures such as iv, v, vi, x

Fidelity, high: HF, hi fi

Fifty: L

Finally: may refer to way a word ends

Financial: see under 'coins', 'currency' and 'pay'

First: may refer to first part of a word

First class: AI, A, ace, top, star

Fish: those most frequently appearing in crossword puzzles include: bass, bream, brill, carp, char, chub, clam, cod, crab, dab, dace, dory, eel, haddock, hake, halibut, herring, limpet, ling, mullet, perch, pike, plaice, prawn, ray, roach, salmon, sardine, shrimp, skate, snail, sole, tench, trout, tunny, turbot, whiting

Five: v

Five hundred: D

Flag: iris; droop

Fleet: RN

Flier: pilot, PO *or* possibly a bird (see list under 'birds')

Flight: could be stairs, or staircase

Flower: possibly a watercourse that 'flows', e.g., a river as Don, Exe, Wye (see list under 'rivers') *or*, more probably, a bloom. Flowers most often blooming in crossword puzzles include: arum, aster, bluebell, clover, cowslip, crocus, daisy, flag, iris, lily, lotus, lupin, mallow, may, mimosa, musk, oxlip, orchid, pansy, pea, peony, pink, poppy, rose, tansy, tulip, viola, violet

Fool: ass, dope, dupe, lout, oaf

Football (body): FA, RU

Force, Air: RAF; (crime prevention) police; (military) Army, BEF; (naval) RN, fleet

Foreigner: alien, *or* possibly 'Dane', 'Slav', 'Finn', etc.

Foreign Office: FO

Form: class, shape

Form of: possibly indicates an anagram (e.g., 'form of bread . . .' could be 'debar' or 'bared')

Former: ex, often used as prefix (e.g., 'Former turn' could be 'ex-act'; 'news media, formerly' might be 'ex-press')

Forty: XL

Four: iv

France, in: often refers to word in French. See following

French: possibly a word written in French, e.g.:
    'a' French, un, une
    'the' French, le, la, les
    'some of the' French, de, de la, du, des
    French agreement, 'oui'; refusal, 'non'
    Frenchman, M; Frenchwoman, Mme; miss, Mlle
    French noble/royalty: Duc, conte, roi, reine
    French coins: franc, louis, cent
    Road in France, rue
    French farewell, adieu

Frenzied, Frenzy: could indicate an anagram, letters being mixed *frenziedly* (e.g., 'I appear torn in a frenzy . . .' could make 'preparation')

Frequency: (high) HF; (very high) VHF

Fresh, afresh: might indicate an anagram, letters being arranged *afresh* (e.g., 'freshly cured, so . . .' could become 'coursed')

Friday: Fri

Friend: pal, ally

From: might indicate an anagram, one word being made *from* the letters of another (e.g., 'Couples from Paris' could make 'pairs')

Front: van

Fruit: those most often used in crossword puzzles include: almond, apple, apricot, banana, cherry, citron, clove, damson, date, fig, lemon, lime, mango, medlar, nut, nutmeg, olive, orange, pear, plum, quince, walnut

Fuddled: could indicate an anagram, the spelling of one word being *fuddled* into another (e.g., 'a real Scot, fuddled . . .' could make 'escalator')

Furies, the: Alecto, Megaera and Tisiphone

G

Gallery: possibly Tate; (of theatre) gods

Gamble: bet, wager, dice

Gardening tools, implements: hoe, fork, spade, roller, rake, mower

Gem: the precious stones and gems found most often in crossword puzzles are: agate, amber, diamond, emerald, garnet, marble, opal, ruby, zircon

General: gen

Gentleman: gent, Mr, Sir *or* foreign courtesy titles for gentlemen such as Don, Dom, M., Signor, Senor, Herr, etc.

German: (man) Herr, Fritz, Hans
(woman) Frau, Fraulein
(title) graf
(article) der
(town) often Essen

Get, gets, getting: often means that one letter, syllable or word *gets*, or joins, another (e.g., 'I'm getting role . . .' could give 'impart' (I'm–part))

Ghastly: might indicate an anagram, the mis-spelling of the required word being *ghastly* (e.g., 'Ghastly Miss Kate . . .' could produce 'mistakes')

Girl: lass, miss, she, her *or* the name of a girl, e.g., Ann, Anna, Emma, etc. (see list under 'names')

Go, goes, going, going to: often means that a letter, syllable or word *goes to*, or joins, another (e.g., 'a railway system going to the Orient . . .' could produce 'abreast' (a–BR–East))

Go, gone, adrift, mad, haywire, etc.,: probably indicates an anagram (e.g., 'artist's gone haywire . . .' could become 'Tsarist')

Golf, golfer, golfing: reference may be to 'tee' or 'iron'

Gold: au, or

Good: OK; (French) bon *or* Good man, probably refers to 'st', abbreviation for saint *or* Good Book, NT, OT, Bible

Graduate: BA, MA, BSc, DSc, etc.

Grasp, -ed, -ing, -s: possibly indicates one group of letters *grasps*, or encloses, another (e.g., 'bin grasped by comer' makes 'combiner' (com–bin–er))

Gratitude: ta

Grave inscription: RIP

Gravity: g, (specific gravity) sg

Great: gt

Greek: Gk

Greek letters: alpha, beta, gamma, delta, epsilon, zeta, eta, theta, iota, kappa, lambda, mu, nu, xi, omicron, pi, rho, sigma, tau, upsilon, phi, chi, psi, omega

Grip, -ped, -ping, -s: possible indicates that a group of letters is *gripped* by another (e.g., 'Fred grips mixed gin . . .' could be 'fringed' [fr(ing)ed])

Grow, -ing, -er, -s: see under 'flower', 'fruit', 'tree'

Grumble: grouse, nag

Gunners: RA

Gunpowder: TNT

Gypsy: nomad, rover, roamer

H

Hail: Ave, Hi, Ho, Ahoy

Hampshire or Hants town: often Liss

Haphazardly: often indicates an anagram (e.g., 'treads haphazardly' could give 'stared')

Hard: (pencils) h

Harpies: Aello, Ocypete, Celaeno, Podarge

Has: may indicate that an abbreviation or word *has*, or has taken on, another, or their synonyms (e.g., 'low dog has debts . . .' could be 'curious' ['cur–IOUs'])

Hashed: might indicate an anagram, the spelling being *hashed into something else* (e.g. 'hashed stew . . .' could give 'west')

Have: see 'has'

Haywire: might indicate an anagram (e.g., 'acts gone haywire . . .' could give 'cats')

Haze, Hazy, Hazily: possibly indicates an anagram, the spelling having become *hazy* (e.g., 'She's in haze . . .' could give 'shines')

Head: (of body) top, capital *or* (of organization) boss, master, dir (director) man, manager *or* (geographical) ness *or* might mean the 'head', or first, letter of a word (e.g. 'Tom's head . . .' could be 'T')

Headland: ness, cape

Heaps: lots, many, piles *or* possibly a number indicating many, e.g., C, D, M

Hear, I hear, we hear: probably means that the answer could sound like a differently-spelt word (e.g., 'Crew had a meal, we hear . . .' could give 'eight', that is the rowing eight, or crew, which *sounds* like 'ate' or had a meal)

Heart: the middle, centre, or *heart* of a word, sometimes a letter sometimes a syllable (e.g., 'a' is the *heart* of 'Paris'; 'lib' is the *heart* of 'calibre')

Heart, losing, probably indicates that the central part, letter, or syllable, of a word must be deleted (e.g., 'Fakir losing heart . . . ' could be 'fair'; '. . . heartless calibre . . .' would leave 'care')

Hearten, give heart to: may indicate that a word is to be extended by having additional letters inserted into its heart (e.g., 'Boer, taking the Italian to heart . . .' could become 'boiler' ['Bo–il–er'])

Heating, central: ch

Heath: (conservative leader) often 'Ted'

Heather: ling, Erica

Heavenly: (bodies, body) possibly a star or planet; (signs) probably one of the Zodiac; see also under 'Zodiac'

Height: h, ht

Held: see 'hold'

Helium: he

Hero: possibly VC, MC, etc.

Hertfordshire town: probably Ware or Tring

Hesitates, with hesitation: may denote use of 'er' or 'um'

Hide, hiding, hides: sometimes indicates that one word or group of letters is *hiding* another (e.g., 'Man is hiding Niki . . .' would give 'manikin')

Higgledy piggledy: probably indicates an anagram (e.g., 'coating all higgledy piggledy . . .' could give 'allocating')

Highway: possibly road, rd, M

Hill: tor

Hint: tip, cue

Hold, -ing, -s: possibly indicates that a group of letters *holds* another, or its synonym (e.g., 'alternative held by man . . .' could give 'morale' [m–or–ale])

Hold up, holding up, held up: may indicate that in a Down solution the lower half of the word is holding *up* another (i.e., read backwards)

Home, at home: in

Hollow: could indicate the insertion of an 'o', meaning 'nothing', into a word (e.g., 'a hollow buy . . .' could produce 'buoy')

Holy man: probably st (saint)

Honour: may be from Honours List, such as OM, OBE, CH, etc.

Horrible, -y: could indicate an anagram, a word respelt *horribly* (e.g., 'horrible brat . . .' could give 'bart')

Horse: nag, gee gee

Horsepower: hp

Host: possibly a crowd, represented by Roman number, e.g., C, D, M

House: (upper) Lords; (lower) Commons

Hot and cold: h c

Hotchpotch: probably indicates an anagram, the spelling of one word being a *hotchpotch* of another, (e.g., 'a hotchpotch of arts . . .' could give 'tsar', 'star' or 'rats')

Hour: h, hr

Hue: see under 'colour'

Hug: May indicate that a group of letters or word is *hugging* another (e.g., 'Tod, hugging last message . . .' could give 'tripod' [i.e., T(R.I.P.)od])

Huge: OS

Hundred, -s: C, CC

Hungry: possibly a noun with the insertion of 'o', meaning 'nothing' (e.g., 'Hungry Bob . . .' could become 'boob', i.e., Bob with nothing in him)

Hush: sh

Hydrogen: H

I

I am, I had, I have, I will: I'm, I'd, I've, I'll

Imperial: imp

Implement: see under 'gardening', 'music' and 'tool'

In: could mean that a group of letters or word is *in* another (e.g., 'ten in pot . . .' could give 'potent')

Incoherent, -ly: might indicate an anagram, suggesting *incoherent* spelling of the answer (e.g., 'raves incoherently . . .' could give 'saver')

Indisposed: ill, sick; (be) ail, ailing

Information: inf, gen, news

Initial, -lly: probably refers to first letters or syllable of a word

Insect: often ant or bee. Insects or grubs most frequently found in crossword puzzles include: ant, bee, beetle, bug, cicada, drone, earwig, flea, fly, gnat, grub, hornet, larva, locust, louse, maggot, midge, moth, spider, termite, tick, tsetse, wasp, weevil

Instance, for: eg

Instrument: tool; see also under 'music'

Intelligence: (agent) spy; (dept) MIV, CIA; (quotient) IQ

International Organization: UN, UNO

Investigators: (dept) CID

Invest: possibly verb, lay siege to

Invests, investing: might indicate that one word surrounds another by *investing* or laying siege to it (e.g., 'army investing our . . .' could give 'armoury')

Ireland: Eire

Irishman: Paddy, Pat

Irish towns or counties: often mentioned in crossword puzzles are Sligo, Mayo, Cork, Tipp., Tyrone, Kildare, Limerick, Down

Iron: (verb) smooth, even; (in golf) club

Isaiah: Is, Isa

Island: isle, ait, islet *or* possibly name of island, such as Man, Mull, Rhum, Wight, CI, IoW, IoM, Lundy, Capri, Elba, RI, Crete, Malta

Israel, in: see under 'Jewish'

Italian: (man) signor; (woman) signora, signorina; (leader) Duce

It: (Italian vermouth)

J

January: Jan

Jerk: twitch

Jewel, jewellery: see under 'gem'

Journal: diary, magazine, mag

Judge: trier, try

July: Jul

Jumbled: possibly indicates an anagram, the spelling of the answer being *jumbled* into something else (e.g. 'jumble sale . . .' could give 'leas' or 'seal')

Jumper: possibly pullover, cardigan, sweater, etc., *or* creature that jumps, e.g., flea *or* a well-known athlete

June: Jun

Junior: jr, jnr, minor, son

K

Key: (musical) A B C D E F G, major, minor

Kilometre: km

King: r, rex

Kiss: x

Knave: J, Jack, rogue, scamp

Knight: kt, sir

Knit, -ted, -ting, -s: could indicate an anagram, the letters of one or more words being *knitted* into another (e.g., 'bent on knitting . . .' could make 'bonnet')

Knot, -ted, -ting, -s: might mean an anagram (e.g., 'knotted ropes . . .' could give 'spore', 'pores' or 'prose')

Knock about, out: KO *or* could indicate an anagram (e.g., 'idler so knocked about . . .' could give 'soldier')

L

Label: tab, tag

Labour: lab, toil

Laboratory: lab

Lacking, lacks: might suggest a word needs to *lack* some of its letters to produce another (e.g., 'Bedlam, lacking 550 . . .' could give 'beam' [i.e., without DL])

Lake: L, mere, tarn

Lancashire town: probably Bury, Leigh or Wigan

Language: tongue, often Erse

Last, at last: often indicates the final letter or syllable of a word (e.g., 'sacrifice is delayed at last' could be 'immolate', i.e., 'late' *at last*)

Last word: often amen

Late: d, dec

Late Monarch: often (Queen) Anne

Lately: (i.e., not any more) ex

Lawman, lawyer: (American) DA

Lead: (in the) van; (metal) pb

Leader: head, chief, capt., duce, pm, primate

leads, leader, leading: possibly refers to first syllable or letter of a word (e.g., 'Army's leader' could be 'A')

Leaf: (page) p, (folio) fo, fol

Learned: (person) usually one with a degree, such as BA, MA, or prof, don, etc.

Learner: L, tyro (tiro)

Learning: lore

Leave, -s, -ing: may refer to a letter or letters *leaving* a complete word to make a different one (e.g., 'abstainer leaves bottle . . .' would make 'bole' [i.e., no TT])

Left: l

Left wing: lab, soc

Letters: mail, post; see also under 'Greek'

Lettuce: cos

Level: even
Liberal: lib
Lieutenant: lieut, lt
Light: beam, ray
Lines: possibly poetry; rails; or airlines (see under 'air')
Linesman: could be poet (one who writes 'lines'), see also under 'poet'
Liquid: ale, beer, gin, rum, tea, water, etc. *or* (measure) nip, tot, gill, pt, pint, qrt, gall
List: rota, roster, roll *or* lean, tilt, cant, slant
Little: often refers to an abbreviation (e.g., 'little mountain' becomes 'mt'; 'little street' becomes 'st', etc.) *or* may refer to children or juveniles (e.g., 'little man' or 'little person' could be 'son', 'tot', 'nipper', 'baby'; 'little sister' might be 'sis', etc.) *or* might refer to young animals (e.g., 'little tiger' could be 'cub', 'little Alsatian' might be 'pup', etc.) *or* often used as a diminutive of a christian name, (e.g., 'Little Edward' frequently becomes 'Ted' or 'Ed', 'little Thomas' is 'Tom', 'little Diana' very often 'Di', little Sarah is sometimes abbreviated to Sal, and so on)
Load: (weight) usually cwt or ton, tons; *or* (carries load of) could suggest that part of a *down* answer 'carries' upper part of the word
Local: inn, pub, tavern
Locality: region, area; or often a postal district in towns and cities, such as EC, WC, NE, NW, SE, SW
Lock: (of hair) tress
Lodger: pg
Long: yearn; (long time) era, age, eon
Look: lo! see! peer, peep, eye, espy
Looker: possibly eye
Lop: may indicate that a word must be 'lopped' by having one or more letters cut off to shorten it and so make another word (e.g., 'lopped hazel' would leave 'haze')
Lose, losing, loses: often indicates that a word loses some of its letters to make another word. 'Loses head' could indicate it loses first letter (e.g., 'Stan loses head . . .' would give 'tan'); 'loses heart' would indicate the word loses part of its central construction (e.g., 'learner loses heart . . .' gives 'leaner'); 'loses tail' would probably indicate removal of last one or two letters (e.g., 'newt losing its tail . . .' gives 'new'). Or the word might lose random letters to leave another complete word (e.g., postmaster losing Matt's letters . . .' leaves

'poser'; and 'disparity losing pits' components . . .' leaves 'dairy' or 'diary')

Lots: many, probably indicates L, C or D (Roman numerals)

Loud: f, ff

Louder: cres.

Love: O, nil, nothing (tennis score)

Loveless: may indicate the removal of 'o' from a word (e.g., 'loveless Tory . . .' would leave 'try')

Low: (cattle sound) moo

Lower: possibly one that lows, e.g., cow, herd

Lowdown: (slang term for information) gen, inf, info, tip, news

M

Mad, madly: could indicate an anagram, the spelling having gone *mad* (e.g., 'mad hatter . . .' could give 'threat')

Magazine: mag

Make, -s, making, made: usually indicates an anagram, one word *making* another (e.g., 'hears Lear making . . .' could produce 'rehearsal')

Main: often reference to sea

Main Force: RN, Navy

Majesty, His/Her: HM

Man: he, him, male, mr; (Isle of) IoM

Manufactured: see 'made'

Many: probably quantity represented by Roman numeral, L, C, etc.

Manuscript, -s: MS, MSS

March: mar

Mariner: AB, Jack, Tar, sailor, Capt.

Married: wed, m

Mashed: might indicate an anagram, the spelling being mashed into another word (e.g., 'mashed grub . . .' could give 'burg')

Master: (of Arts) MA, teacher, boss; (hunt) MFH *or* (skilled) ace, star, dab, expert

Material: fabric; rep, wool, satin, cotton, serge, voile, silk, ninon, crepe, velvet *or* word is possibly 'material' for an anagram (e.g., 'I pen art material for . . .' could give 'painter')

Measure: (printer's) em, en; (cloth) el, ell; (length) in, ft, yd, mm, m, km, f; (area) rood, acre; (liquid) gill, pt, quart, qt, gall, litre, l; (weight) dram, ounce, oz, stone, quarter, qtr, cwt, ton

Medical: (officer) MO, MOH; (organization) BMA; (service) NHS

Medical man; Medicine, man of: dr, gp, MB, MO, MOH, doc, FRCP, FRCS

Meet, -ing, -s, met: usually denote one syllable or word *meeting* another, or their synonyms, to form new words (e.g., when 'Quiet king meets little devil . . .' you could get 'shrimp' [i.e., sh–R–imp])

Member: (limb) arm, leg; (of Parliament) MP

Messy: probably infers an anagram, a spelling being a *messy* version of another (e.g., 'messy plates . . .' could give 'petals')

Mile: m

Military man: GI, Tommy, cpl, sgt, rsm, lt, cap, col, maj, gen, co, cgs, cigs

Mince, -d: usually denotes an anagram, the word having been *minced* to produce another (e.g., 'rum pie minced . . .' could produce 'umpire')

Mineral: ores most frequently found in crossword puzzles include: agate, alum, borax, coal, emery, flint, grit, mica, nitre, ore, pitch, potash, silex, silica

Minus: frequently means that a word is minus, or without, a letter or syllable, to produce a different word (see under 'lose' and 'leave')

Mischief, up to, -maker: usually imp or scamp

Missing: may denote part of a word is missing, to produce another word (e.g., 'furnished missing urn . . .' would produce 'fished')

Mistake: err, error, sin

Mistakenly: might indicate an anagram (e.g., 'mistakenly desire evil . . .' could give 'deliveries')

Mister: M., Mr

Mixed up, mixture: probably indicates an anagram, the spelling being *mixed* to produce a different result (e.g., 'mixed up broth . . .' could produce 'throb')

Model: poser; (model worker) ant, bee

Modern: mod, in

Monarch: r, rex, king, ER, queen

Monday: Mon

Money: see under 'coins' and 'currency'

Monsieur: M

Month: mon, or abbreviation of calendar month, generally Jan, Feb, Mar, Apr, May, Jun, Jul, Aug, Sep, Oct, Nov, Dec

Morning: am

Morning, in the: may mean that a word is literally written *in* 'am', or between its letters (e.g., 'in the morning, airline . . .' could produce 'abeam' [i.e. 'a–BEA–m'])

Mosaic: might imply an anagram, the letters being arranged into a *mosaic* of a new word (e.g., 'mosaic of R.S. pictures . . .' would give 'scriptures')

Mother: ma, mater, mum, dam

Motor: car, engine

Motoring organization: AA, RAC

Motorist: driver

Motorway: M, M1

Mountain, -s: mt, mount, Alps, range, ben, height

Mountain pass: col

Muddle, -d, -s: probably indicates an anagram, the spelling being a *muddled* version of another word or words (e.g., 'men muddled with arts . . .' could give 'smarten' [i.e., men/arts mixed up])

Multitude: host, mob, crowd, D, M, MM

Muses: Calliope, Clio, Euterpe, Melpone, Thalia, Erato, Terpsichore, Polyhymnia, Urania

Music, -al, -ally: (notes of scale) A B C D E F G (tonic sol fa) do re ra mi fa so la si or te (music notation) breve, semi-breve, minim, crotchet, quaver, semi-quaver

Musical directions: p, pp, f, ff, forte, cres, dim, lente, viva, all

Musical instruments: those seen most often in crossword puzzles include: banjo, 'cello, clarinet, cymbal, drum, fiddle, fife, flute, harp, horn, lute, lyre, oboe, organ, piano, sax, trumpet, ukelele, viol, viola, violin

Musicologists, composers: Those appearing most often in crossword puzzles include: Arne, Bach, Brahms, Chopin, Clementi, Coates, Delius, Elgar, Handel, Haydn, Holst, Ludwig (Beethoven), Mahler, Purcell, Ravel, Rossini, Strauss, Sullivan, Weber

Musketeers: Athos, Porthos, Aramis

N

Name: n

Names: *Boys' Names* likely to occur in crossword puzzles include: Al, Alf, Alfred, Art, Arthur, Adam, Alan, Andy, Andrew, Angus, Ben, Bert, Bill, Bob, Brian, Carl, Carlos, Chas, Cecil, Chris, Clive, Claud, Colin, Dai, Dan, Dave, Dick, Des, Desmond, Don, Ed, Edgar, Eddie, Eric, Ernest, Ernie,

Edward, Ewan, Evan, Felix, Frank, Fred, Geo, George, Glen, Glyn, Hal, Hans, Hugh, Ian, Ivan, Jan, Jack, Jim, Jo, Jock, Joe, John, Jon, Jose, Jules, Ken, Keith, Kit, Lance, Larry, Len, Leo, Les, Leslie, Lew, Louis, Mac, Mark, Martin, Max, Mick, Mike, Miles, Nick, Noel, Nye, Ossie, Oswald, Owen, Pat, Paul, Pete, Peter, Perry, Phil, Ray, Rex, Rob, Robin, Rod, Roddie, Ron, Sam, Sandy, Sid, Simon, Stan, Steve, Ted, Terry, Tim, Tom, Tony, Vic, Victor, Will, Wm, William, Wally, Walter, Zog

Girls' Names likely to occur include: Alice, Amy, Ann, Anna, Anne, Bella, Belle, Bet, Bette, Betty, Bess, Carrie, Claire, Clara, Clare, Cleo, Ciss, Cora, Connie, Con, Di, Dora, Dot, Dolly, Edie, Elsie, Emma, Ethel, Eva, Eve, Fanny, Fay, Faith, Flo, Flora, Floss, Freda, Gert, Gertie, Gwen, Helen, Hilda, Hope, Holly, Ida, Irene, Iris, Isabel, Isobel, Ivy, Jane, Jean, Jenny, Jess, Joan, Josie, Joy, Jo, Julia, Julie, June, Kate, Kathy, Katie, Kay, Kit, Kitty, Laura, Lena, Linda, Lorna, Lucy, Maggie, Mai, May, Mary, Meg, Moll, Molly, Nan, Nell, Nellie, Nora, Norma, Olive, Pearl, Peg, Peggy, Penny, Poppy, Pansy, Pat, Pru, Ray, Rene, Rita, Rose, Ruth, Ruby, Sal, Sally, Sue, Susan, Serena, Tess, Tessa, Teresa, Tilly, Tina, Trixie, Una, Vera, Verity, Vi, Violet, Viv, Vivienne, Wanda, Winnie, Wynne

National: nat

Nationalized Transport: BR

Navy: RN

Needs remaking, revising, re-ordering, etc,: indication of an anagram, the word needing remaking to form a different one (e.g., 'a sarong needs remaking . . .' will produce 'angoras')

Neighbourhood: see under 'local, locality'

New, anew: possibly implies an anagram, spelling needing to be rearranged to make a *new* word (e.g., 'new design . . .' could make 'deigns')

News: gen, inf, par, item

Newspaper: press, edition, issue

Never-never: hp

Nickel: ni

Nil: o, nix

Noble, nobleman: Duke, Earl, Count, Lord, Baron, Peer

Nomadic: possibly indicates an anagram, the letters wandering *nomadically* to form something else (e.g., 'nomadic hikers . . .' could make 'shrike')

Non-flier: possibly emu

Noon: (before) am; (after) pm

Norfolk town: usually Diss

Note: (musical) A B C D E F G *or* do, doh, re, ra, mi, fa, so, la, si, te

Nothing: o, nil, nix

Notice: ad, advert

Nought: see 'nothing'

Noun: n

Novelist: those most frequently appearing in crosswords include: Austin, Bronte, Gide, Hugo, Poe, London, Zola (see also under 'writers')

November: Nov

Now: inst, AD

Number: no.; *or* one, two, three, etc.; *or* i, ii, iii, iv, v, vi, X, L, D, C, M

O

Obstacle: bar

October: Oct

Odd, oddly: may indicate an anagram, the spelling of the required solution being *oddly* presented (e.g., 'oddly thin clog . . .' could give 'clothing')

Of the (French): de, de la, du, des

Officer: CO, C in C; lt, cap, maj, col, brig, gen, FM, cdr, Capt, adml; (non-commissioned) nco, cpl, sgt, rsm; (medical) MO, MoH

Old, Olden: may refer to obsolete or outdated speech (e.g., 'your old' could be 'thine'; 'old you' might be 'thou', 'thee', 'ye'; 'from where old . . .' might be 'whence') *or* aged, ex

Old Boy: OB

Old City: probably Ur

Old Money: s or bob (shilling); d (penny)

On board: might be a word written *between* s s (steamship) (e.g., 'big ones may be hot on board . . .' could be 'shots' [i.e., s–hot–s])

One: a, an, l, ace

One French: un, une

One time: once, former, ex

Opposite: converse, *or* may literally mean an antonym (e.g., 'just the opposite . . .' could be 'unjust', 'unfair', 'take the opposite . . .' might be 'give')

Order: see 'honours'
or (Postal) PO

Order, re-order, put in order: possibly denotes an anagram the *order* of a word or words being changed to find the solution (e.g., 'Nice eels ordered . . .' could give 'licensee')

Order, Head of: possibly refers to religious order, Head being Abbot

Ordinary Seaman: OS

Ore, -s: see under 'Mineral'

Organize, -d, -ing, -ation: might indicate an anagram, the letters being *organized* into a different order (e.g., 'earth re-organized . . .' or 'organization of earth . . .' could give 'heart')

Organization: (international) UN, ILO; (European) EEC; (motoring) AA, RAC; (medical) BMA; (union) TUC

Orient: E, East

Out: could mean one letter or section of a word is taken *out*, leaving another (e.g., 'decamped, with tents out . . .' would leave 'deed') *or* might indicate an anagram, the spelling being *out* (e.g., 'spine out . . .' could give 'pines')

Outsize: OS

Overturned: in a Down solution, might indicate that a word has different meaning when turned upside-down, i.e., read upwards (e.g., 'overturned trams . . .', read upwards, would give 'smart')

Owe, owing: IOU, IOUs

P

Pack: (possible reference to hunting) hunt, MFH

Page: p, pp

Painter: (artist) RA, PRA; (organization) RA, RI *or* possibly the name of an artist, those most often seen in crossword puzzles including: Hals, Lely, Lowry, Manet, Monet, Orpen, Renoir, Rubens, Spencer, Turner, Whistler

Pair: pr *or* might be two appearances of one word, (e.g., 'pair of tins' might be 'cancan')

Palaver: ado, fuss

Pale: ashen, wan

Palindrome: a word which reads the same backwards or forwards (e.g., minim, tenet, rotor, madam, civic, refer)

Panama: Pa

Paris, in, Parisian: often another way of indicating a French translation of a word (e.g., 'good morning in Paris . . .' could be 'bonjour', or 'a Parisian husband . . .' could be 'mari')

Part: bit, role, some, piece *or* possibly part of a word having a separate meaning from the whole (e.g., 'Viceroy's chilling part . . .' might be 'ice')

Party: do, fete, binge; (political) Cons, Tory, Lab, Soc, Lib, C, L

Pass: col

Pay: fee, salary, wage; (freight) cod; (tax) paye

Peak: tip, ben, tor, summit, top, apex, Everest

Peculiar: odd *or* might indicate an anagram, the spelling of the solution being *peculiar* until re-arranged (e.g., 'cans it in a peculiar way . . .' could be 'antics')

Pedestrian: ped

Pence, penny: (new) np, p; (old) d

Perform, -er: act, actor, do, doer

Period: stop; (in time) age, eon, AD, BC; (short or little) tic, sec, min, hr

Periodical: journal, magazine, mag

Permit: let, allow

Personality: id, ego

Philadelphia: Pa

Philosopher: possibly Plato, Russell

Phone: ring, call

Physical exercise, training: PT

Piano: p, pp

Pieces, in: possibly an anagram the word being broken up in pieces and reassembled (e.g., 'pieces of china . . .' could make 'chain')

Pious: pi, holy

Place, all over the: probably an anagram (e.g., 'tread all over the place . . .' could be 'rated' or 'trade')

Planet: Earth, Jupiter, Mars, Mercury, Neptune, Pluto, Saturn, Uranus, Venus

Plant: see under 'flower', 'fruit', 'tree', 'vegetable'

Play: drama, act

Plead: O, beg

Plutonium: pu

Poem: ode, verse, stanza; (heroic) epic

Poetically: often a poet's abbreviation of a word (e.g., 'over' becomes 'o'er'; 'never' becomes 'ne'er')

Point: dot, tip, N S E W

Poison: possibly as (arsenic)

Pole: N S; rod, perch; post, shaft

Police: force; (dept) CID; (man) pc, bobbie, copper; (vulgarly) fuzz

Popular: pop

Population: pop

Port: (at sea) L; (drink) wine; (harbour) Deal, Dover, Calais, etc.

Portuguese title: Dom

Possibly: may indicate an anagram, a spelling *possibly* making something else (e.g., 'possibly tried . . .' could become 'tired')

Postal Order: PO

Postal service: Mail

Post Office: GPO, PO

Postscript: PS, PPs

Pound: l, ll, lb

Power, electric, measurements: amp, ampere, ohm, watt volt

Precious stones: see under 'gems'

President: P, pres

Present time: now, inst, AD

Press: (assocns) AP, PA, IPA

Prices & Incomes Board: PIB

Priest: pr, fr, rev, Eli

Primate: ape

Prime minister: pm

Prince, -ss: P, HRH

Prison: gaol, jug, quod, can, stir

Prisoner: (of war) pow *or* possibly one word is the *prisoner* of, or imprisoned within, another (e.g., 'aunt the prisoner of Ted . . .' or 'Ted imprisons aunt . . .' could make 'taunted')

Prison sentence: stretch, time

Private: pte

Produce, product, production: may indicate an anagram, one word being the *product* of the letters of another (e.g., 'dramatic production of regal kin . . .' could produce 'King Lear')

Professional: pro

Professor: prof

Promontory: ness, head, cape

Pronoun: he, she, it, they, we, them, me, us, etc.

Props up: in a down solution, usually indicates that lower half of word *props up* the first half which can be read upwards a well as downwards (e.g., if 'dipole' were written downwards 'Pole' might be said to be propping up basic man, or 'id' written upwards)

Prophet: seer; (or, often) Amos, Isaiah, Is, Isa

Public house: inn, local, pub

Public relations: PR

Public Relations Officer: PRO

Pulled apart: possibly implies an anagram, a word having been pulled apart to remake another (e.g., 'thread pulled apart...' could make 'dearth')

Punch: (final) KO

Pupil: scholar, iris

Put in: might mean a word or letter is inserted into another (e.g., 'ten put in pot...' would give 'potent')

Put in order: may denote an anagram, letters being *put in order* differently (e.g., 'file put in different order...' could produce 'life')

Q

quart: qt

quarter: qr; (compass quarters) N S E W

Queen: R, ER, Q; (if notably dead) Anne

Queer, -ly: may indicate an anagram (e.g., 'Queer Miss Day...' could give 'dismays')

Quiet, -ly: p, pp, sh, hush

R

Radical: rad, root

Radiotelephone: RT

Radius: r

Rage, raging: might indicate an anagram, the letters of a word raging about wildly (e.g., 'raging for minutes...' could give 'misfortune')

Ragged, raggedly: possibly suggests an anagram (e.g., 'ragged cuffs...' could produce 'scuff')

Railway: rly; (organization) BR; (old, or former, rail company) LMS, GWR, LNER, SR, GN

Rambling, raving: might indicate an anagram

Range: (possibly mountains) Alps, Pennine, Urals, Andes

Rascal: rogue; (little) imp, scamp

Rasher: possibly bacon

Rate: (speed) mph, knot, kn

Ransacked: could indicate an anagram, the word being *ran-*

sacked into a changed appearances (e.g., 'wardrobes ransacked . . .' could give 'bare sword')

Recall, -ed, -ing, -s: possibly means a word is to be *called back*, or to change direction, i.e., reverse spelling (e.g., 'Neil recalled . . .' could give 'lien')

Receptacle: those occurring most frequently in crossword puzzles include: bag, bin, bowl, box, cup, dish, jug, pan, pot, sac, sack, tin

Record: disc, LP, tape, log, file

Refreshment: ale, cider, gin, rum, tea, lager, beer, brandy, wine, soup

Refuse: no, non, not, nay, noes *or* rot, rubbish, trash, tripe

Regina: Q, R

Rehash, -ed: might denote an anagram, the spelling of a word having been *rehashed* into something else (e.g., 'rehashed stew . . .' could be 'West' or 'wets')

Relation, -s, relative: kith, kin, sis, sister, bro, brother, ma, mum, mater, dam, pa, pop, pater, dad, father, sire, uncle, aunt, niece, nephew, twin

Religious: (person) nun, monk, priest, etc.; (house) convent, abbey, priory, monastery; (head) abbot, superior

Reorganized: probably denotes an anagram, the letters of a word having been *reorganized* into another (e.g., 'a throne reorganized . . .' could make 'another')

Repeat, -ed: might indicate a word or phrase which *repeats* syllables (e.g., 'dodo', 'Isis', 'Baden-Baden')

Replaced: may indicate an anagram *or* indicate that one group of letters or syllable has been replaced by another to change a word (e.g., 'listener replaced small works in dry surroundings . . .' could make 'dreary' instead of 'dropsy' [i.e., dr–ear–y/dr–ops–y])

Reply: ans

Representative: rep, agent; (in Parliament) MP; (at conference) del

Reptile: adder, anaconda, asp, boa, cobra, python, salamander, serpent, snake, viper

Reset: might denote an anagram, the order of the letters of a word being *reset* to make another: (e.g., 'tool having been reset . . .' could make 'loot')

Request: ask, beg, O, Oh,

Reshaped: could indicate an anagram (e.g., 'reshaped dome . . .' could give 'mode')

Resort: spa, haven *or* possibly the name of a health or seaside resort such as Hythe, Hove, Dover, Bath, Nice, Cannes *or* might indicate an anagram, the letters being resorted into another word (e.g., 'resorting letters . . .' could give 'trestle')

Resting, at rest: RIP, asleep, naps, nods, lies, prone *or* might imply that a word or group of letters is inserted into 'bed' or 'cot' (e.g., 'a prophet at rest . . .' could be 'belied' [i.e., b–Eli–ed])

Retire, -d, -s, -ing: might refer to a word spelt in reverse (e.g., 'Kay retires . . .' could give 'yak') *or* when meaning somebody has retired to bed, could be letters or word inserted into 'bed' or 'cot' (e.g., 'hero, retired . . .' could give 'cheroot' [i.e., c–hero–ot])

Retired: retd

Return, -ed, -s, -ing: could indicate a word must be spelt backwards (e.g., 'net returns . . .' could give 'ten')

Reverend: rev

Reverse, -d, -s, -ing, reversal: might indicate that the spelling of a word must be reversed (e.g., 'reversing tram . . .' could give 'mart')

Revolution: possibly an anagram, a *revolution* of the letters producing another word (e.g., 'red power revolution . . .' could give 'powderer')

Revolutionary: red, rebel, Marxist

Revolver: weapon *or* possibly article that revolves, such as turnstile, rotor, axle, top

Rex: king, r

Rhode Island: RI

Right: r, rt

Ring: O, call

River: those most seen in crossword puzzles include: Arun, Avon, Axe, Cam, Congo, Dee, Don, Elbe, Ems, Ebro, Exe, Indus, Isis, Marne, Mole, Nile, Oder, Ouse, Po, Rhine, Rhone, Seine, Somme, Stour, Test, Trent, Ure, Usk, Volga, Wey, Wye

Road: rd, st, ave

Roaming: might suggest an anagram, the spelling *roaming* into other words (e.g., 'mad son, roaming . . .' could give 'nomads')

Roman: possibly Latin word in general use; (law) lex; (peace) pax

Round: O, ring *or* might mean that a group of letters or word is *round* another (e.g., 'ask Bet round . . .' could be 'basket' [i.e., B–ask–et])

Row: noise, din, uproar; line, tier; scull, oar

Rowers: oarsmen, crew, eight

Royal: R; (Academy) RA; (Artillery) RA; (Cipher) ER; (Engineers) RE; (Highness) HRH; (Royal Mail Steamer) RMS; (Society) RS

Rubbish: rot, tosh, refuse, trash

Ruffian: rogue, (little) imp, scamp

Rugby: (football) RFC, RU

Ruin, -ed, -s: may denote an anagram, the word being in *ruins* before being rebuilt into the answer (e.g., 'Oslo in ruins . . .' could be 'solo')

Runs, runner: possibly liquid that runs (see 'river')

Run wild: probably denotes an anagram, the spelling *running wild* (e.g., 'Deer running wild . . .' could give the solution 'reed')

Ruler: king, queen, emperor, emp, dictator

Russia: USSR

Russian: red, Ivan, Serge; (fighter) Mig

S

Sailor: AB, Jack, OS, tar, capt, adml

Saint: st

Sappers: RE

Saturday: Sat

Scale: do, re, ra, mi, fa, so, la, si, te

Scan: con

Scatter, -ed, -s, -ing: probably indicates an anagram, the letters of words being *scattered* to form something else (e.g., 'scatter scatter . . .' could give 'TT races')

Scholar: pupil; schoolboy

School: sch, Eton, Harrow, etc.

Science, scientist: sc, Bsc; Lister, Newton, Darwin, Curie, etc.

Scot, Scots, Scotsman: mon, Ian, Jock, Mac, Sandy, Bruce *or* possibly a word as a Scot might pronounce it (e.g., 'Scots own . . .' might be 'ain'; 'Scottish surprise . . .' could be 'Och!')

Scrambled: could denote an anagram, letters being *scrambled* into another word (e.g. 'iced and scrambled . . .' could give 'candied')

Sculptor: probably the name of a well-known sculptor, e.g., Rodin, Moore, Angelo

Sea, at: possibly an anagram *or* might be a word or letters inserted between 'ss' (steamship) indicating one being afloat

Second: s, sec; (class) B

Secretary: sec

Seize, -d, -s: may indicate that a group of letters or word encloses, or *seizes* another (e.g. 'apple seized by theologian ...' could give 'dappled' [i.e., D–apple–D])

Self: ego, id

Self-centred, selfish: (person) egoist, egotist

Senior: snr, major

Senior Citizen: OAP, elder

September: Sep, Sept

Serpent: asp, boa, adder, cobra, viper, snake; (see also 'reptiles')

Serpentine: see under 'twist'

Service: (winner) ace *or* possibly one of armed services such as RN, RAF; (former women's) ATS

Shade: hue (see also under 'colour')

Sheep: ewe, ram, teg

Shilling: (old) s, bob

Ship: mv, ss, boat, liner, cruiser, trader, brig, ketch, sloop, yacht

Shivery: brr

Short, -ly: soon, anon; *or* may mean something is spelt 'in short' or abbreviated (e.g., 'Bedfordshire shortly . . .' could be 'Beds'); (see also under 'little')

Shrub: see under 'flower' and 'tree'

Sickly: ill, ail, ailing *or* could indicate an anagram, the letters being in *sickly* array (e.g., 'Emil's sickly ...' could give 'smile')

Side: team, eleven, XI, fifteen, XV

Sign: omen; (heavenly) one of astrology. See under 'Zodiac'

Silence: hush, sh

Silencer: gag

Silver: ag

Simpleton: ass, dope, dolt, dupe, fool, sap, sop

Singer: alto, alt, tenor, bass, soprano, sop, contralto

Sister: sis

Six: vi

Skill: art

Sleep: doze, kip, nod, nap, zz

Slippery: probably related to 'eel' or 'ice'

Slipping: may denote an anagram, the letters *slipping* about (e.g., 'kids slipping ...' could give 'skid')

Smash, -ed, -ing, -s: could indicate an anagram, a word being *smashed* and reassembled (e.g., 'smashing times . . .' could give 'smite', 'mites' or 'items')

Smooth: level, even, iron, plane

Smug: pi

Snake: see 'serpent' and 'reptiles'

Socially acceptable: U, OK

Society: soc

Soft, -ly: p, pp, sh

Some: possibly a small number indicated by spelt numerals (e.g., six, ten) or by roman numerals, (e.g., iv, v, x, etc.)
or may indicate part of a word (e.g., 'some drumming' could be 'rum')

Somehow: probably denotes an anagram (e.g., 'Somehow enraged . . .' could give 'angered')

Somersaulted, -ing, -s: in a Down clue, probably indicates that a word can be read the other way up, or head over heels (e.g., 'Enid somersaulting . . .' could give 'dine')

Soprano: sop

Son: (of, Welsh) Ap; (of animals), possibly cub, foal, pup, etc.

Song: aria, air, lay, ditty

Songster: possibly a bird (see under 'birds')

Sort, sort of, sorting: possibly indicates an anagram, (e.g., 'sort of gear . . .' could give 'rage')

Sound, -ly, sounds like: probably a word is spelt as another is pronounced: (e.g., 'Soundly whacks . . .' could be 'wax')

South: S

Spanish: (the) el; (gentleman) senor, Don; (lady) senora, donna; (hero) Cid

Speak: orate

Specific gravity: sg

Speed: rate, mph, knot, kn

Spill, -ed, -ing, -s, spilt: might denote an anagram, the letters being *spilt* into a different order (e.g., 'spilling wines . . .' could give 'swine' or 'sinew')

Spirit, -s: genie, sprite, ghost, spectre; gin, whisky, rum, Scotch, brandy, meths, alcohol

Split, -s, -ing: maybe a group of letters or word is inserted into another, *splitting* it (e.g., 'we split sled . . .' would make 'slewed', 'file being split by theologian . . .' would give 'fiddle' [i.e., fi–DD–le])

Spoil: mar

Spoils: mars, booty, loot, swag, prize

Spring: spa; leap, jump

Stairs, staircase: could be flight
Stamped addressed envelope: SAE
Standard: norm, par; flag
Starboard: right, rt, r
Starting price: sp
State: say, aver *or* possibly one of the United States, which abbreviated, are: Ala, Alas, Ariz, Ark, Cal, Colo, DC, Conn, Del, Fla, Ga, Ida, Ill, Ind, Ia, Kan, Ky, La, Me, Md, Mass, Mich, Minn, Miss, Mo, Mont, Neb, Nev, NH, NJ, NM, NY, NC, ND, Okla, Oreg, Penn, RI, SC, S Dak, Tenn, Tex, Ut, Vt, Va, Wash, W Va, Wis, Wyo
Steamship: ss
Stew, -ed, in a: probably denotes an anagram, the letters being all stewed up (e.g., 'Crimean st in a stew . . .' could give 'miscreant')
Stir, -red, -ring, -s: possibly indicates an anagram (e.g., 'races stirred up . . .' could give 'acres')
Stone: see under 'gem' and 'mineral'
Storyteller: liar, novelist, romancer, taleteller, author
Straightened: may indicate an anagram, the spelling having been *straightened* out to give another word (e.g., 'bent it, straightened . . .' would give 'bitten')
Strange: odd *or* could indicate an anagram (e.g., 'strange diet . . .' could give 'edit', 'tide' or 'tied')
Stray, -ed, -ing, -s: might denote an anagram, the letters *straying* into another spelling (e.g., 'strayed from stream . . .' could give 'form master')
Street: st, rd
Stretch: eke; (in prison) term, spell, time
Strike: hit, lam; (lightly) tap, pat
Striker: batsman
Strong: (loud) f, ff
Stud: boss
Study: con, scan; den
Suburb: (of London) often Tooting, Acton, Ealing
Sulphur: s
Summer: (British-time) BST; adder
Sun: sol
Sunday: Sun
Support, -er: prop, fan, seconder; (art) easel
Supports, supporting: In a Down clue may refer to a group of letters or word supporting, or holding up another
Swallow, -ed, -ing, -s: may indicate that one group of letters or

word takes in, or *swallows*, another (e.g., 'Bing has swallowed less . . .' could give 'blessing' [i.e., B–less–ing])

Swimmer: possibly a water creature. (See under 'fish')

Swirling: probably denotes an anagram, the letters *swirling* into another word (e.g., 'with swirling capes . . .' could give 'paces', 'space' or 'scape')

T

Tail: possibly the last letter of a word (e.g., 'tiger tail . . .' might be 'r')

Tailed: a group of letters or word may be *tailed*, or followed by another (e.g., 'ran, being tailed by detectives . . .' might give 'rancid' [i.e., ran–CID]) *or* (when 'topped and tailed') the first and final letters of a word might be lopped off (e.g., 'berry topped and tailed . . .' could be 'err')

Take, -ing, -n, -s: often refers to letters or syllables *taking*, or joining on to, others, to form a longer word (e.g., 'rev father takes gloomy dean . . .' could give 'fringe' [i.e., fr–Inge]; 'pet taken by car . . .' could give 'carpet')

Takes in, taken in: may refer to a group of letters or word being *taken in* by another (e.g., 'good man taken in by jeers . . .' could give 'jesters' [i.e., je–St–ers])

Take up, takes up: may refer, in a Down clue, to one group of letters or word being added to another, the last being read *upwards* in the clue (e.g., 'car takes up nob . . .' would give 'carbon')

Take out, takes out: probably refers to the removal of a group of letters or word to produce a smaller complete word (e.g., 'French gentlemen taken out of summit . . .' would give 'suit' [i.e., su(MM)it])

Tale: story, romance

Taleteller: sneak, romancer, novelist *or* possibly the name of a novelist (e.g., Dickens, London)

Tangled: possibly denotes an anagram, the spelling being *tangled* (e.g., 'tangled nets . . .' could give 'nest' or 'Sten')

Tavern: inn, pub, local

Tea: cha, char, cuppa

Teatime: iv, v, four, five

Team: side, eleven, xi, xv, fifteen

Tee: T

Teetotal: TT

Telephone: ring, call

Television: TV; (authority) ITA; (company) ATV

Ten: x

Tennis: (Assoc) LTA

Territorial Army: TA

Testament: will; (New) NT, (Old) OT

Thanks: ta

That is: ie

The: (French) le, la, les; (German) der; (Italian) il; (Spanish) el

Theologian: DD

Thermal (unit): BTU

Though: yet, but

Thoughts: ideas; (second) PS, PPS

Thousand, -s: M, MM

Threesome: trio

Thursday: Th, Thur

Time: t, tick, sec, min, hr, day, wk, month, yr, age, era, eon, BC, AD

Tiny: see under 'little'

Title: Lord, Lady, Sir, Count, Baron, Earl, Duke, Prince, etc.

To: often means one word, syllable or letter comes *to* or joins another (e.g., 'artist to chant . . .' could be 'rasing' [i.e., RA–sing])

To and fro: may infer that a word will read the same whether to or fro, or backwards and forwards (e.g. rotor, radar, civic)

To-do: fuss, bother

Tome: vol, volume, book, bk

Tongue: possibly reference to foreign language

Tool: awl, hoe, jig, axe, saw

Topsy turvy: possibly denotes an anagram (e.g., 'topsy turvy dial . . .' could be 'Dali' or 'laid')

Tossed, tosses about: probably indicates an anagram, the spelling being *tossed* into different position (e.g., 'vessel, tossed about . . .' could give 'selves')

Town: English towns most often found in crossword puzzles include Liss, Hove, Ely, Diss, Loo, Rye, Ryde, Dover, York, Stoke

Transport: car, cab, van, cart, train, bus, bike, ship, boat, rail, plane; BR, rly; (air) BEA, BOAC, BA, KLM, SAS, PanAm, ElAl, etc.

Trapped: possibly denotes one group of letters or word is *trapped* within another (e.g., 'cad trapped in Dee . . .' could give 'decade')

Tree: those most often seen in crossword puzzles include:

abele, acacia, alder, almond, apple, ash, aspen, banana, banyan, bay, beech, birch, box, cedar, cork, damson, ebony, elder, elm, fig, fir, hazel, holly, larch, laurel, lemon, lilac, lime, linden, maple, may, nut, oak, olive, orange, osier, palm, pear, peach, pine, plane, plum, poplar, prunus, rowan, rubber, spruce, sumac, sumach, teak, upas, walnut, wattle, willow

Trial: test, exam

Trier: judge

Try: essay, judge, test

Trouble: irk, bother, ail; ado, fuss

Troubled: could indicate an anagram, the spelling being *troubled* (e.g., 'troubled ride . . .' could be 'dire')

Tuesday: Tues, T

Turn, -ed, -ing, -s: could indicate that a syllable or word *turns* round, to be read backwards (e.g., 'tide turns . . .' could give 'edit'; 'Sid turns to count . . .' could give 'discount')

Twice: possibly a syllable used *twice* to make a word (e.g., 'river is twice . . .' could be 'Isis' [i.e., Is–is])

Twist, -ed, -ing, -s: could denote an anagram, the word being *twisted* to spell another (e.g., 'serpent twisting . . .' could give 'present')

Twitch: tic

Tyro: L

U

Uncertain,-ly: could imply use of 'er' or 'um'

Uncle: (American) Sam

Union: wedding, *or* possibly trade union such as NUR, NUM, NUT; (organisation) TUC *or* might indicate the union of two or more syllables or words (e.g., 'cat and bird union . . .' could give 'tomtit')

United Kingdom: UK

United Nations: UN

United States: USA, US (see also under 'states')

Unknown: anon, x

Unruly: could denote an anagram, the word being *unruly* (e.g., 'unruly state of teens seen . . .' could make 'Tennessee')

Untidy: probably infers an anagram (e.g., 'Untidy Ned . . .' would give 'end' or 'den')

Untwisted: another anagram, probably (e.g., 'untwisted rope for . . .' could give 'reproof')

Up: possibly denotes that a word may be read upwards, if in a Down clue (e.g., 'Nur is up to . . .' would read 'run' downwards – probably lower half of a solution)

Up against: usually means a group of letters or syllable is *up* against, or adjoins, another (e.g., 'run up against gravity shortly . . .' could give 'rung')

Upper, Upper class: U

Upset: probably means an anagram, the letters of a word having been *upset* to make another (e.g., 'pans upset . . .' could give 'snap')

Utensil: see under 'tool', 'receptacle' and 'vessel'

V

Variation, varied, variety: probably denotes an anagram, the spelling being *varied* into another word (e.g., 'dance variation . . .' could be 'caned')

Vegetable: veg. Those most often seen in crossword puzzles include bean, beet, cabbage, carrot, celery, cos, cress, endive, greens, kale, leek, lentil, oats, onion, parsnip, pea, potato, sprout, spud, swede, tomato, turnip

Vehicle: cab, car, cart, coach, dray, gig, bus, tram, van, growler (see also under 'transport')

Versus: v, anti

Very: v

Vessel: ship, ss, mv, boat, brig, ketch, yacht, skiff, sloop, liner, cruiser; pot, pan, can, tin, cup, bowl, basin

Veterinary: vet

Viewer: eye

Virginia: Va

Voice: say, speak, utter; (singer) bass, tenor, alto, baritone, contralto, soprano; (Roman) vox

Volt: v

Volume: vol, book, tome; (see also under 'measure')

Vote: x

Vulgar, -ly: may denote slang or colloquial speech (e.g., 'money, vulgarly speaking . . .' could be 'dough'; 'vulgar food . . .' might be 'grub', 'bangers', 'nosh', etc.)

W

Wager: bet, stake, gamble

Wanderer: nomad, gypsy, rover, roamer, stray, tramp

Warmth: (thermal) BTU; (central heating) ch

Water: Aq

Way: M, road, rd, street, st, path, ave, route; (by way of) via; manner

Wednesday: Wed

Wee, weeny: see under 'little'

Week: wk

Weekday: S M T Tu W Th Fri, Sat, Sun, Mon, Tues, Wed

Weight: dram, oz, lb, qtr, cwt, ton, gramme, gm, kg, mg

Weird: odd, uncanny; or possibly denotes an anagram

Welsh: (man) Dai, Taff, Taffy, Evans, Evan, Owen, Tudor, Jones, Lewis; (woman) Megan, Blodwen; (son of) ap; (town) Barry, Swansea; (river) Usk, Taff; (county) often Glam

Wet: possibly means a noun is enclosed within another meaning a lake, sea, river, etc.

Whim: fad

Whirling: possibly indicates an anagram, the spelling of one word or more *whirling* to make another (e.g., 'whirling rope for . . .' could give 'reproof')

Wight, Isle of: IoW

Wicked: bad, foul, evil, vile; (man) rogue, devil, fiend

Wickedly: possibly an anagram, something being *wickedly* spelt (e.g., 'devil wickedly . . .' could give 'lived')

Wild, -ly: probably denotes an anagram, a word being *wildly* spelt to make another (e.g., 'wild lion . . .' could give 'lino' or 'loin')

William: Will, Wm, Bill, Tell

Willing: perhaps somebody making a will, e.g., testator

Wind, -ing, -s: probably denotes an anagram, the letters of a word *winding* differently (e.g., 'winding lane . . .' could give 'elan' or 'lean'; 'one lane winding eastwards . . .' might give 'Elaine [i.e., ela–i–nE])

Wine: (French) vin; (Italian) vino; or Barsac, Beaune, Burgundy, Chablis, Champagne, Chianti, Claret, Graves, Hock, Macon, Madeira, Marsala, Moselle, Port, Reisling, Rioja, Sauternes, Sherry, Tokay, Vermouth

Wing: (left) Lab, L, Soc, S; (right) Cons, C, Tory

Winger: possibly a flier (see under 'birds') or might be name of prominent footballer

Within: might denote a group of letters or word is *within*, or enclosed by, another (e.g., 'listener within Martin's home . . .' could give 'nearest' [i.e., n(ear)est])

Woman: she, her, lass, miss, mrs. madam, wife, mme; *or* possibly the name of a girl (see under 'names')

Word: (last) amen

Work: toil, opus, op

Worker: hand; (-s) staff, men; (model worker or busy worker) ant, bee

Writer: nib, pen, pencil, quill, stylo; *or* poet, author, novelist, essayist, scribe; *or* a writer by name, e.g., Sterne, Addison, Poe, Hugo, Gide, Austin, London, Zola, Bronte, Yeats, Twain, etc.

Writings: MS, MSS

Wrong, -s: sin, err, error, tort, crime

or might denote an anagram, the solution being wrongly spelt in the clue (e.g., 'dire wrong . . .' could give 'ride')

Y

Yard: y, yd, CID

Yarn: tale, story, thread

Year: yr

Yearn: long

York, New: NY

You and me/I: we, us

You old: thou, thee

Your old: thine

Young: may imply something small (see under 'little')

Z

Zero: O, nil

Zodiac: (signs of) Aquarius, Pisces, Aries, Taurus, Gemini, Cancer, Leo, Virgo, Libra, Scorpio, Sagittarius, Capricorn